The Paris Review

Founded in 1953.

The Paris Review is published quarterly by The Paris Review, Inc. Vol. 38, No. 139, Summer 1996.
Business Office: 45–39 171 Place, Flushing, New York 11358 (ISSN #0031-2037). Paris Office:
Harry Mathews, 67 rue de Grenelle, Paris 75007 France. London Office: Shusha Guppy, 8 Shawfield
St., London, SW3. US distributors: Random House, Inc. 1(800)733-3000. Typeset and printed in
USA by Capital City Press, Montpelier, VT. Price for single issue in USA: $10.00. $14.00 in Canada.
Post-paid subscription for four issues $34.00, lifetime subscription $1000. Postal surcharge of $8.00
per four issues outside USA (excluding life subscriptions). Subscription card is bound within magazine. Please give six weeks notice of change of address using subscription card. *While The Paris
Review welcomes the submission of unsolicited manuscripts, it cannot accept responsibility for
their loss or delay, or engage in related correspondence. Manuscripts will not be returned or
responded to unless accompanied by self-addressed, stamped envelope. Fiction manuscripts
should be submitted to George Plimpton, poetry to Richard Howard, The Paris Review, 541 East
72nd Street, New York, N.Y. 10021.* Charter member of the Council of Literary Magazines and
Presses. This publication is made possible, in part, with public funds from the New York State Council
on the Arts and the National Endowment for the Arts. Second Class postage paid at Flushing,
New York, and at additional mailing offices. **Postmaster:** Please send address changes to 45-39
171st Place, Flushing, N.Y. 11358.

THE PARIS REVIEW
announces a
Prize for Poetic Drama

In preparation for our upcoming theater
issue, *The Paris Review* will award a prize
for the finest previously unpublished
poetic drama. Manuscripts may be no
longer than thirty pages. The winning
piece will be published in *The Paris
Review*; its author will receive $2,000.

Submissions must be accompanied by an SASE
and be postmarked no later than
November 1, 1996.
Submissions should be sent to:
Poetic Drama Prize
The Paris Review
541 East 72 St.
New York, NY 10021

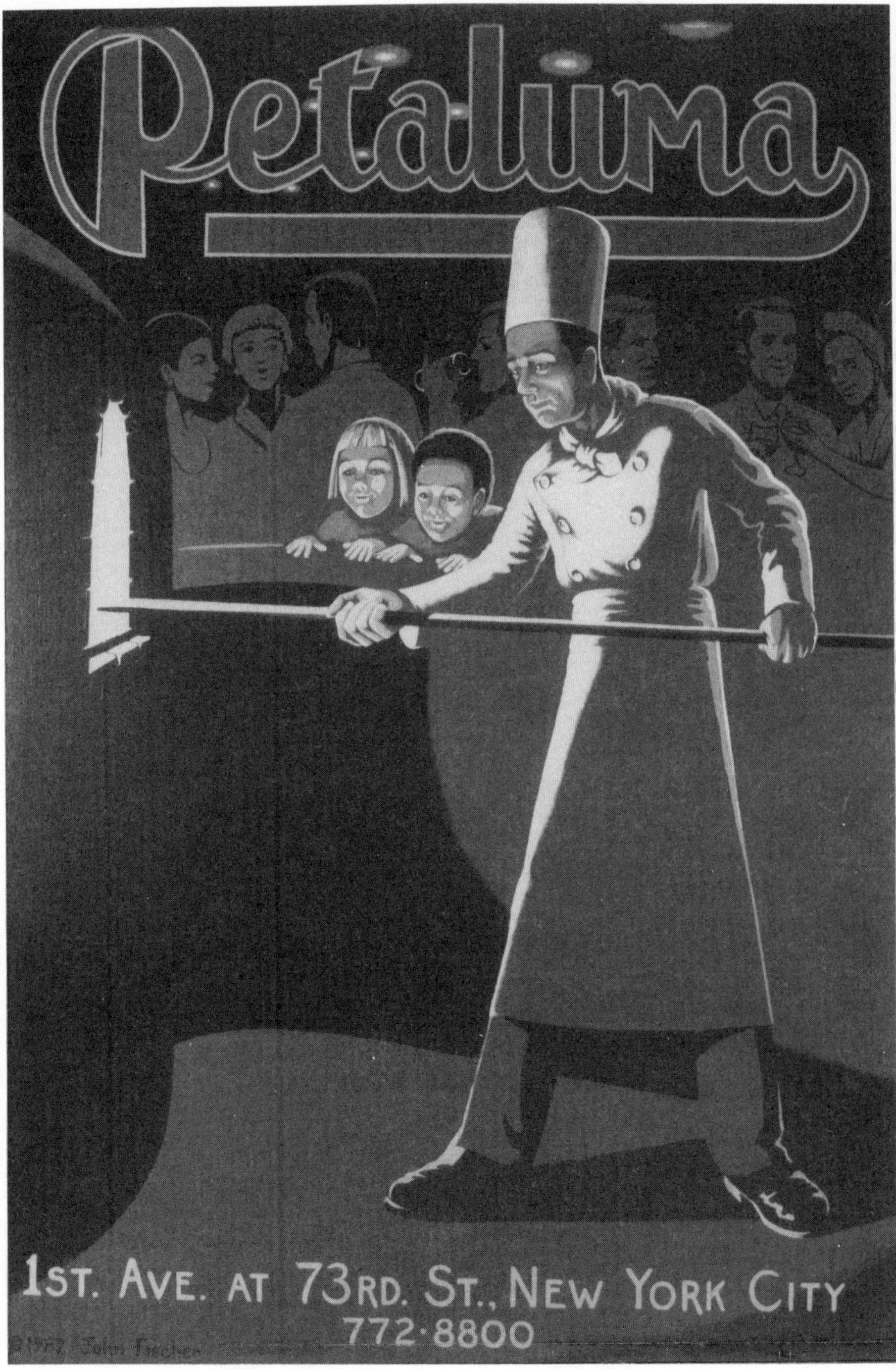
Petaluma
1st. Ave. at 73rd. St., New York City
772·8800

The
Paris
Review

Editorial Office:
541 East 72 Street
New York, New York 10021
HTTP://www.voyagerco.com

Business & Circulation:
45-39 171 Place
Flushing, New York 11358

Distributed by Random House
201 East 50 Street
New York, N.Y. 10022
(800) 733-3000

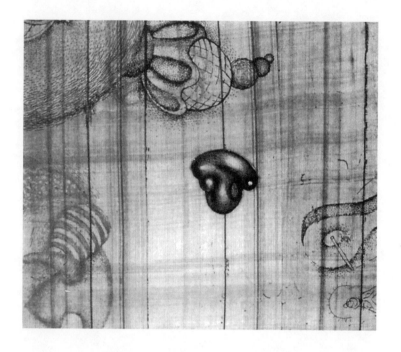

Table of Contents illustration by Leona Christie, *Under a Lens of Certain Manufacture #1*, 1995, intaglio and ink drawing. Cover by Donald Sultan, *Orange Flowers*, 1996, silk screen. Frontispiece by William Pène du Bois.

Number 139

A Reunion:
Cocteau and Picasso

James Lord

. . . A couple of days later I went to Vallauris, climbed the
overgrown slope to Picasso's ugly little house, and found the
family, including Paulo, the son of the artist's first marriage,
just finishing lunch at about half past two. I was aware that
if one were to find them at home, this was the most likely
hour. Picasso knew that I had been seeing Cocteau and soon
inquired about him. "Not too dopey from smoking?" he sar-
castically inquired. "Not to my knowledge," I answered, reflecting that Picasso might have refrained from sarcasm, having
been in his youth heavily addicted to the pipe. I said that
Jean wanted to come and pay his old friend a visit and asked
what day would be convenient. Any day would be convenient,
Picasso replied, but there were days when he was absent, so
callers had to take their chances. If I wanted to escort Cocteau
to Vallauris, I should consult my lucky stars to find the right
moment. This certainly did not constitute an invitation, even
less a specific appointment, but with Picasso, protocol
stemmed exclusively from his dicta. I said we'd see. After a

while we went to his studio on the other side of town to observe what progress had been made on the life-size likeness of a goat made from scraps of junk picked up here and there by the artist and stuck together with plaster. Picasso was very pleased with it. But then . . . when was he not pleased with something wrested from oblivion by his hands? As for myself, I disliked the goat from the beginning and still do.

To tell Jean exactly what had been his old friend's reaction to the prospect of an imminent visit was not an appealing option. So I said only that the absence of a telephone in Picasso's house made it difficult to settle on a specific day, because the artist was subject to unpredictable commitments, such as Communist meetings, though I didn't believe for a minute that Picasso could be led to comply with any agenda except his own. Jean took this in with composure and said that Picasso was like the law that governed the universe: incomprehensible and inexorable, to be accepted without understanding by one and all, including Picasso himself. The daily sunrise itself possessed no more self-determination than Picasso when he stood before a blank canvas, brush in hand. So we would willingly put our faith in the goodwill of gravity and go to Vallauris three days later, a Thursday, stopping en route to have lunch at La Bonne Auberge, a luxurious restaurant on the highway between Nice and Antibes.

Jean and I had a jolly lunch at La Bonne Auberge. I was flattered and entertained to hear all his stories, though I realize that they would have been exactly the same had his guest been someone else—a shepherd, policeman, shoeshine boy, archbishop, circus acrobat, cardsharp, or what have you. I felt no conviction that the advent of James Lord in Cocteau's life would modify its landscape by so much as the addition of a single blade of grass. He talked about Proust, Nijinsky, opium, Picasso, his marriage to the Russian ballerina Olga Kokhlova, Matisse, and Braque, and the Empress Eugénie, who had ended her days not far from where we sat, about Modigliani and the hardships of an artist's life, about his own diseases, his solitude, his battle to survive the war with language. I tried to say the right thing at the right time. Not that I believed it made a scrap of difference. But I think I did tolerably well, because Jean bestowed a few smiles upon me and kept on talking. It was just two when we finished. Francine's car and chauffeur waited outside. Half an hour later we were in Vallauris.

Picasso, Françoise and the two children were still at table under the grape arbor. Exclamations of surprise, pleasure and warm remembrance of bygone comradeship were immediate. The two men embraced. Invited to sit down and have a cup of coffee, we did. Picasso said he'd heard Cocteau was present somewhere along the coast but hadn't known how to get in touch with him. Jean said the same thing. Then wasn't it a spendid bit of luck that little Lord had come along to bring together, after far too long a separation, a pair of friends who had meant so much to each other? How many memories! Those luminous Roman afternoons in 1917. Diaghilev, Stravinsky, and Bakst, Selisburg, the bon vivant lawyer. The studio in the Via Margutta. *Parade*. Their youth. And now they stood on the threshold of old age. No, no, no, said Jean. The paintings, the poetry would live forever in the midmorning of youth. All very well, murmured Picasso, but the body does not obey. Consider Cheops. Relatively speaking, he had been present on earth but a moment before, and now nobody living could tell you the color of his eyes.

Just when the conversation had become worth remembering and recording, it was interrupted by the arrival of an uninvited Scandinavian photographer who wanted to take some pictures of the famed painter. Until his last years, Picasso rarely turned away photographers, because they were important to the propagation of his legend. On this occasion he willingly posed with Paloma in his arms, then ostentatiously introduced Cocteau to the photographer, who was delighted at his luck in finding two celebrities on hand instead of one, both of them, as it happened, only too happy to submit to the interrogation of the camera. By chance I had one with me as well and took a couple of snaps of the celebrated couple, all smiles. When the photographer had finished, Picasso took Jean by the arm and suggested that they go to visit his studio. This invitation seemed to include me as well, also Françoise, who left her children in the care of the *femme de ménage*. The photographer had clearly not been invited, but he asked, with what I considered some brashness, whether he might come along, and Picasso agreed on condition that he ride with Jean and me. Picasso's car led the way and we followed.

The studio, on the other side of town, had several rooms, one for painting, another for drawings and the largest for scuplture. We visited the painting studio first. When I was present for showings of recent work, Picasso often asked me to carry outside into the sunshine the two paintings that pleased him most, both of them versions of works by other artists. The first, and, I felt, the better, was based on a Courbet of two women voluptuously drowsing beside a river; the other was a "copy" of a supposed self-portrait by El Greco. After these pictures had been admired and carried back inside, we passed into the room where a great heap of drawings lay helter-skelter on a large table. To have touched any of them would have seemed presumptuous, and as Picasso did not pause we followed along while he made his way toward the open door of the next room, which was the sculpture studio. The anonymous photographer, however, was not intimidated. Picking up from the table a large and beautiful drawing in red crayon of a centaur and a woman, he said to Picasso, "Did you do this?"

Smirking at the obvious, Picasso said, "Yes."

"Well, do you mind," inquired the photographer, "if I take it along as a souvenir?"

The rest of us, aghast at such unthinkable effrontery, held our collective breath, expecting an outburst of indignation from the artist. But he liked caprice and contradiction. "Take it, of course," Picasso said. "People claim I'm stingy, but it always gives me pleasure to offer a little souvenir to someone who likes what I do."

The presumption of the photographer was not yet satisfied, "Then would you sign it?" he asked.

"Why not?" cried Picasso, snatching a crayon from the table. And he did.

Then we all filed into the sculpture studio, bemused by
what everyone except the photographer knew to have been
an astonishing exception to the prevailing law of Picasso's studio. Not that he wasn't generous. He gave close friends and
mistresses quantities of drawings and paintings. But to respond with grace to the blunt request of a stranger was decid-
edly not his usual practice (though, to be sure, he had once
made a similar exception for me).

Since my last visit, the goat had acquired more plaster round
its belly, which had originally been a wicker basket, and an
anus made of the bent bottom of a tin can. There were plenty
of other things to admire as well. The sculpture studio, where
Picasso had been expending most of his energy over the past
months, was a sort of Ali Baba's cave of his works, large and
small. As we stood around, admiring and exclaiming, Picasso
suddenly turned to Cocteau and said, "Well, Jean, since I'm
handing out gifts, I don't want to neglect an old friend like
you. Not after all that we've been through together. Let's see
what I can find."

He turned away toward the rear of the studio, where a shelf
along the back wall was piled with objects. Jean, Françoise,
the photographer and I waited with impatient anticipation.
Since he had made an admirable gift to a total stranger, it
seemed natural that he should outdo himself for an old friend.
And he did—but as only Picasso might have succeeded in
outdoing Picasso.

He turned toward us, smiling, with his right hand out-
stretched, grasping an object which he held out toward Jean,
who took it as we all craned forward to see what it was. And
what it was was what nobody but Picasso—or a child of five
or six—could ever have made into something that looked like
a Picasso: a roughly triangular scrap of broken pottery from
which a handle protruded like a grotesque nose, on either
side of which the artist had painted a black dot with a straight
line underneath, making of the discarded fragment a ludicrous
semblance of some approximate human or animal counte-
nance. In all the studio there can hardly have been an object
so preposterously devoid of beauty, novelty or artistic interest

of any kind whatsoever. Cocteau looked at it with an expression of fastidious disgust, as if he had been handed a scrap of excrement, which was very nearly what, in fact, had occurred. And for once he was left speechless.

Surely sensitive to the significance of his talkative friend's silence, Picasso said, "Look on the inner side. It's signed."

And, indeed, on the curved inner side of what had once been a cheap casserole of some kind, Picasso's signature was largely inscribed.

Then Cocteau found his voice. "Ah, Pablo," he murmured, "what you've given me is evidence that there must be life outside our solar system. This fragment is like a telegram from another world, the world where everything is created from nothing, and your name on it proves that life goes on forever, that Cheops dwells among us still, and I wager you could tell that the color of his eyes is exactly the same as yours, since both of you can see beyond the confines of creation."

"Well, I knew that that was just the thing for you," said Picasso.

Françoise observed that it was time for both her and Pablo to get to work, which I recognized as the tactful means of ending a highly awkward encounter. So we went back to the car. The photographer said good-bye and sauntered down the hill, his beautiful drawing held carefully against the breeze. Jean kissed Picasso and Françoise on the cheeks and got into the car. I did likewise and we drove away, having been in Vallauris little more than an hour.

For some moments Jean said nothing as we drove down toward the main highway. I knew the outburst was coming. He sat very straight and stared at the preposterous object in his hand. I was extremely ill at ease, because for some irrational reason I felt at fault for what had happened. The longer Jean remained silent the more tense the atmosphere within the car became, so finally I blurted, "That was abominable."

Jean glanced at me, shaking his head. "No," he said, "that was simply Picasso. Abominable, yes, but he remains Picasso, immutable, absolute creation. I couldn't tell you all the abominable things he's done. A god, you know, can be a monster.

Consider Apollo torturing the miserable Marsyas to death merely because he wanted to play the flute."

But he did tell me of many unkind and cruel things Picasso had done, many to women but more than enough to men, during the years he'd spent in Paris. As he spoke he became angry, his voice grew shrill, and he waved the scrap of pottery in the air for emphasis. I was almost alarmed, feeling still that somehow I must be to blame for what had happened. I didn't record all the misdeeds attributed by Jean to his old friend, but I did write down that Picasso had once broken the leg of his ballerina wife by striking her with a chair during an altercation. I've since been told that, although Olga did at one time suffer a broken leg, Picasso probably was not responsible for it, however emphatically Jean that afternoon insisted he was. The old story of Picasso's disowning his friend Apollinaire when questioned about the stolen statuettes from the Louvre also came up. It as well is probably untrue. And the allegation that Picasso had not lifted a finger to save his oldest friend, Max Jacob, from the gestapo. There were plenty of other stories, too, enough to occupy the entire time of our drive back to Villefranche. Some of them must have been true, but I couldn't record them all, especially as Bernard continually interrupted me, wanting to know exactly what had happened. The strange thing was that Jean had never once referred to the hideous object given him by Picasso, nor did he later ever mention it, though for some time it sat ludicrously on the mantelpiece in the salon at Santo-Sospir, disappearing only when gifts indescribably finer took its place.

Several days went by before I returned to Vallauris. Picasso's car was not on the road at the foot of the path, and I found the front of the house deserted, the door closed. It was not the first time I'd made the trip for nothing. Still, I thought that the *femme de ménage* might be present and decided to have a look in the kitchen before going to the studio or the pottery, where Picasso often worked in the midafternoon. The kitchen door was at the head of a flight of outside concrete stairs that led up to a terrace. It stood open. Picasso sat alone at the table inside. I said hello. He stared at me for a long minute, then shouted, "How dare you bring that whore to my house?"

Stunned, I stepped backward and muttered some phrase to the effect of not understanding.

At this Picasso leapt to his feet, overturning behind him the chair on which he'd been seated, and shouted, "That whore Cocteau. He never would have dared to come by himself, so he used you. When I think I've treated you like a son, and you do this to me. It's intolerable. I told Françoise you'd fail the test."

"But how could I know?" I stammered. "It was you who told me to go and see him. He was a witness at your wedding. You've known each other for forty-five years."

"That buffoon," said Picasso, "that perfidious arriviste, that vampire. How many young men do you think he's destroyed? Maybe you're one of them. Has he been fucking you?"

"No, he hasn't," I said. "And he's never tried to."

"Amazing," murmured Picasso. "Opium then, I suppose."

"Not at all."

"Well, I can imagine he was pretty enraged by the gift I found for him, wasn't he?"

"He didn't say so. He didn't mention it at all."

"Ungrateful slut!" Picasso exclaimed, picking up his chair and sitting down again at the kitchen table. For some time he sat there in silence, staring at nothing, and it was as if he had ceased to be aware of my presence.

Feeling that it was time to leave, I said, "I'm sorry. I only wanted to please everyone. If it turned out badly, I'm sorry."

"Oh, don't burst into tears," Picasso said calmly. "Here. Come and sit down. Have a glass of wine. You Americans are so sentimental. Maybe that's why you think you should rule the world."

I didn't answer. The two of us sat together quietly for a few minutes, and then the voices of Françoise and the children came from outside. Picasso put his hand over mine. "Don't despair," he said. "What I told you about Cocteau is the truth. You'll find out. But he has a song. If you find the music pleasing for a while, all right. I like it myself sometimes. Now

I must go and put some teats onto my goat. Come back soon."
Then he was gone.

Françoise came into the kitchen with some packages. "Has
he been shouting?" she asked.

"He frightened me," I said.

"He was planning on that. It's what he likes to do. As an
artist, too. Very good at it. But you must never show fear.
Just be yourself, then you're all right. If necessary, you can
walk out and close the door."

Chez Lambert

Jonathan Franzen

St. Jude: that prosperous midwestern gerontocracy, that patron saint of the really desperate. The big houses and big cars here filled up only on holidays. Rain pasted yellow leaves to cars parked in blue handicapped slots. Teflon knees and Teflon hips were flexed on fairways; roomy walking shoes went squoosh, squoosh on the ramps and people movers at the airport.

Nobody laughed at seniors in St. Jude. Whole economies, whole cohorts, depended on them. The installers and maintainers of home-security systems, the wielders of feather dusters and complicated vacuums, the actuaries and fund managers, the brokers and tellers, the sellers of sphagnum moss and nonfat cottage cheese and nonalcoholic beer and aluminum stools for sitting in the bathtub with, the suppliers of chicken cordon bleu or veal Parmesan and salad and dessert and a fluorescently lit function room at $13.95 a head for Saturday night bridge clubs, the sitters who knitted while their charges dozed under afghans, the muscular LPNs who changed diapers in the night, the social workers who recommended the hiring of the LPNs, the statisticians who collated data on prostate

cancers and memory and aging, the orthopedists and cardiolo-
gists and oncologists and their nurses, receptionists and
bloodworkers, the pharmacists and opticians, the performers
of routine maintenance on American-made sedans with incon-
ceivably low odometer readings, the blue-uniformed carriers
of Colonial-handicrafts catalogues and pension checks, the
bookers of tours and cruises and flights to Florida, the projec-
tionists of PG-rated movies at theaters with Twilight Specials,
the drafters of wills and the executors of irrevocable trusts,
the radio patrolmen who responded to home-security false
alarms and wrote tickets for violating minimum-speed post-
ings on expressways, the elected state officials who resisted
property-tax reassessment, the elected national representatives
who kept the entitlements flowing, the clergy who moved
down corridors saying prayers at bedsides, the embalmers and
cremators, the organists and florists, the drivers of ambulances
and hearses, the engravers of marble markers and the operators
of gas-powered Weed Whackers who swept across the cemeter-
ies in their pollen masks and protective goggles and who once
in a long while suffered third-degree burns over half their
bodies when the motors strapped to their backs caught fire.

The madness of an invading system of high pressure. You
could feel it: something terrible was going to happen. The
sun low in the sky, a mockery, a lust gone cold. Gust after
gust of entropy. Trees restless, temperatures falling, the whole
northern religion of things coming to an end. No children in
the yards here. Shadows and light on yellowing zoysia. The old
swamp white oak rained acorns on a house with no mortgage.
Storm windows shuddered in the empty bedrooms. Distantly
the drone and hiccup of the clothes dryer, the moan of a leaf
blower, the smell of apples, the smell of the gasoline with
which Alfred Lambert had cleaned the brush from his morning
painting of the porch furniture. At three o'clock the fear set
in. He'd awakened in the great blue chair in which he'd been
sleeping since lunch. He'd had his nap and there would be
no local news until five o'clock. Two empty hours were a sinus
in which infections raged. He struggled to his feet and stood
by the Ping-Pong table, listening in vain for Enid.

Ringing throughout the house was an alarm bell that no one but Alfred and Enid could hear directly. It was the alarm bell of anxiety. We should imagine it as one of those big cast-iron dishes with an electric clapper that sends school-children into the street in fire drills, and we should imagine it ringing for so many hours that the Lamberts no longer heard the message of "bell ringing" but, as with any sound that continues for so long that you have the leisure to learn its component sounds (as with any word you stare at until it resolves itself into a string of dead letters), instead heard a clapper going ping-ping-ping-ping-ping against a metallic res-onator, not a pure tone but a granular sequence of percussions with a keening overlay of overtones; ringing for so many days that it simply blended into the background except at certain early-morning hours when one or the other of them awoke in a sweat and realized that a bell had been ringing in their head for as long as they could remember; ringing for so many months that the sound had given way to a kind of metasound whose rise and fall was not the beating of compression waves but the much, much slower waxing and waning of their *con-sciousness* of the sound. Which consciousness was particularly acute when the weather itself was in an anxious mood. Then Enid and Alfred — she on her knees in the dining room opening drawers, he surveying the disastrous Ping-Pong table — each felt near to exploding with anxiety.

The anxiety of coupons, in a drawer containing boxes of candles in designer colors, also utensils of pewter and silver in flannel bags. Overlaying these accessories for the dinner parties that Enid no longer gave was a stratum of furtiveness and chaos, because these dining-room drawers often presented themselves as havens for whatever Enid had in hand when Alfred was raging and she had to cover up her operations, get them out of sight at whatever cost. There were coupons bundled in a rubber band, and she was realizing that their expiration dates (often jauntily circled in red ink by the manu-facturer, a reminder to act quickly while the discount opportu-nity lasted) lay months and even years in the past: that these hundred-odd coupons, whose total face value exceeded $60 (potentially $120 at the supermarket on Watson Road that doubled coupons), and which she had clipped months *before* their expiration, had all gone bad. Tilex, sixty cents off. Excedrin PM, a dollar off. The dates were not even *close*. The dates were *historical*. The alarm bell had been ringing for *years*.

She pushed the coupons back in among the candles and shut the drawer. She was looking for a letter that had come by registered mail some weeks ago. She had stashed it somewhere quickly because Alfred had heard the mailman ring the bell and shouted, "Enid! Enid!" but had not heard her shout, "Al, I'm getting it!" and he had continued to shout, "Enid!" coming closer and closer, and she had disposed of the envelope, presumably somewhere within fifteen feet of the front door, because the sender was The Axon Group, 24 East Industrial Serpentine, Schwenkville, PA, and some weeks or perhaps months earlier she had received a Certified letter from Axon that for reasons known better to her than (thankfully) to Alfred she had been too anxious to open immediately, and so it had disappeared, which was no doubt why Axon had sent a second, registered letter subsequently, and this entire circumstance was something she preferred to keep from Alfred, because he got so darned anxious and was impossible to deal with, especially regarding the situation with Axon (which, thankfully, he knew almost nothing about), and so she had stashed the second letter as well before Alfred had emerged from the basement bellowing like a piece of earth-moving equipment, "There's somebody at the door!" and she'd fairly screamed, "The mailman! The mailman!" and he'd shaken his head at the complexity of it all.

She felt sure that her own head would clear if only she didn't have to wonder, every five minutes, what Alfred was up to. It seemed to her that he had become somewhat depressed, and that he ought, therefore, to try to take an interest in life. She encouraged him to take up his metallurgy again, but he looked at her as if she'd lost her mind. (She didn't understand what was so wrong with a friendly suggestion like that; she didn't understand why he had to be so *negative*.) She asked whether there wasn't some work he could do in the yard. He said his legs hurt. She reminded him that the husbands of her friends all had hobbies (David Schumpert his stained glass, Kirby Root his intricate chalets for nesting purple finches, Chuck Meisner his plaster casts of great monuments of the ancient world), but Alfred acted as if she were trying to distract him from some great labor of his, and what was that labor? Repainting the wicker furniture? He'd been repainting the love seat since Labor Day. She seemed to recall that the last time he'd painted the furniture it had taken him only a few hours to do the love seat. But he went to his workshop morning after morning, and after three weeks she ventured in to see how he was doing, and the only thing he'd painted was the legs. After three weeks! And he'd clearly missed a spot on one of the legs! He seemed to wish that she would go away. He said that the brush had gotten dried out, that that was what was taking so long. He said that scraping wicker was like trying to peel a blueberry. He said there were crickets. She felt a shortness of breath then, but perhaps it was only the smell of gasoline and the dampness of the workshop that smelled like urine (but could not possibly be urine). She fled upstairs to look for the letters from Axon.

Six days a week several pounds of mail came through the slot in the front door, and since nothing incidental was allowed to pile up on the main floor—since the fiction of living in this house was that no one lived here—Enid faced a substantial tactical challenge. She did not think of herself as a guerrilla, but a guerrilla was what she was. By day she ferried materiel from depot to depot, often just a step ahead of the governing force. By night, beneath a charming but too-dim sconce at a too-small table in the breakfast nook, she staged various actions: paid bills, balanced checkbooks, attempted to decipher Medicare co-payment records and make sense of a threatening Third Notice from a medical lab which demanded immediate payment of $0.22 while simultaneously showing an account balance of $0.00 carried forward and thus indicating that she owed nothing and in any case offering no address and naming no entity to which remittance might be made. It would happen that the First and Second Notices were underground somewhere, and because of the constraints under which Enid waged her campaign she had only the dimmest sense of where those other Notices might be on any given evening. She might suspect perhaps the family-room closet, but the governing force, in the person of Alfred, would be watching a network newsmagazine at a volume thunderous enough to keep him awake, and he had every light in the family room burning, and there was a non-negligible possibility that if she opened the closet door a cascade of catalogues and *House Beautiful*s and miscellaneous Merrill Lynch statements would come toppling and sliding out, incurring Alfred's wrath. There was also the possibility that the Notices would not be there, since the governing force staged random raids on her depots, threatening to "pitch" the whole lot of it if she didn't take care of it, but she was too busy dodging these raids ever quite to take care of it, and in the succession of forced migrations and deportations any lingering semblance of order was lost, and so the random Nordstrom's shopping bag that was camped behind a dust ruffle with one of its plastic handles semidetached would contain the whole shuffled pathos of a refugee existence— nonconsecutive issues of *Good Housekeeping*, black-and-white snapshots of Enid in the 1940s, brown recipes on high-acid paper that called for wilted lettuce, the current month's telephone and gas bills, the detailed First Notice from the medical lab instructing copayers to ignore subsequent billings for less than fifty cents, a complimentary cruise-ship photo of Enid and Alfred wearing leis and sipping beverages from hollow coconuts, and the only extant copies of two of their children's birth certificates, for example.

Although Enid's ostensible foe was Alfred, what made her a guerrilla was the house that occupied them both. They had always aimed high in decorating it, and its furnishings were of the kind that no more brooked domestic clutter than a hotel lobby would. As without in prosperous St. Jude, so within chez Lambert. There was furniture by Ethan Allen. Spode and Waterford in the breakfront. The obligatory ficus, the inevitable Norfolk pine. Copies of *Architectural Digest* fanned on a glass-topped coffee table. Touristic plunder—

enamelware from China, a Viennese music box that Enid out
of a sense of duty and mercy every so often wound up and
raised the lid of. The tune was "Strangers in the Night."

It's to their credit, I think, that both Lamberts were hope-
lessly ill-equipped to manage such a house; that something
in each of them rebelled at the sterility. Alfred's cries of rage
on discovering evidence of incursions — a Nordstrom's bag surprised in broad daylight on the basement stairs, nearly precipi-
tating a tumble — were the cries of a government that could
no longer govern. It was finance that betrayed him first. He
developed a knack for making his printing calculator spit columns of meaningless eight-digit figures, and after he devoted
the better part of an afternoon to figuring the cleaning woman's social-security payments five different times and came up
with four different numbers and finally just accepted the one
number ($635.78) that he'd managed to come up with twice
(the correct figure was $70.00), Enid staged a nighttime raid
on his filing cabinet and relieved it of all tax files, which might
have improved household efficiency had the files not found
their way into a Nordstrom's bag with some misleadingly ancient *Good Housekeepings* concealing the more germane documents underneath, which casualty of war led to the cleaning
woman's filling out the forms herself, with Enid merely writing
the checks and Alfred shaking his head at the complexity of
it all.

It's the fate of most Ping-Pong tables in home basements
eventually to serve the ends of other, more desperate games.
When Alfred retired he appropriated the eastern end of the
table for his banking and correspondence. At the western end
was the portable color TV on which he'd intended to watch
the local news while sitting in his great blue chair but which was
now fully engulfed by *Good Housekeepings* and the seasonal
candy tins and baroque but cheaply made candleholders that
Enid never quite found time to transport to the Nearly New
consignment shop. The Ping-Pong table was the one field on
which the civil war raged openly. At the eastern end Alfred's
calculator was ambushed by floral-print pot holders and souvenir coasters from the Epcot Center and a device for pitting

cherries that Enid had owned for thirty years and never used; while he, in turn, at the western end, for absolutely no reason that Enid could ever fathom, ripped to pieces a wreath made of pine cones and spray-painted filberts and Brazil nuts.

To the east of the Ping-Pong table lay the workshop that housed his metallurgical lab, the industry underpinning the seamless prosperity of the house above. This workshop was now home to a colony of mute, dust-colored crickets that clustered and roiled in various corners. There was something fetal about these crickets, something provisional. When you surprised them they scattered like a handful of dropped marbles, some of them misfiring at crazy angles, others toppling over with the weight of their own copious protoplasm, which had the color and texture of pus. They popped all too easily, and cleanup took more than one Kleenex. The Lamberts had many afflictions that they believed to be outsized, extraordinary, unheard-of—unmentionable—and the crickets were one of them.

The gray dust of evil spells and the enchanted cobwebs of a place that time had forgotten cloaked the thick insulating bricks of the electric arc furnace, the Hellmann's Real Mayonnaise jars filled with exotic rhodium, with sinister cadmium, with stalwart bismuth, the handprinted labels browned and blasted by the leakage of vapors from nearby glass-stoppered bottles of sulfuric acid and aqua regia, and the quad-ruled notebooks with cracked leather spines in which the latest entry in Alfred's hand dated from that time, nearly twenty years ago, before the spell was cast, before the betrayal. Something as daily and friendly as a pencil still occupied the random spot on the workbench where Alfred had laid it in a different decade; the passage of so many years imbued the pencil with a kind of enmity. Worse than a palace in ruins is a palace abandoned and decaying and untouched: if it were ruined it could be forgotten. A ceramic crucible of something metallurgical still sat inside the furnace. Asbestos mitts hung from a nail beneath two certificates of U.S. patents, the frames warped and sprung by dampness. On the hood of a binocular microscope with an oil-immersion lens lay big chips of peeled paint from the ceiling. The only dust-free objects in the room were a wicker love seat on a dropcloth, a can of Rustoleum and some brushes, and a couple of YUBAN coffee cans which despite increasingly irrefutable olfactory evidence Enid chose not to believe were filling up with her husband's urine, because what earthly reason could he have, in a house with two and a half bathrooms, for peeing in a YUBAN can?

Until he retired, Alfred had slept in an armchair that was black. Between his naps he read *Time* magazine or watched *60 Minutes* or golf. On weeknights he paged through the contents of his briefcase with a trembling hand. The chair was made of leather that you could smell the cow in.

His new chair, the great blue one to the west of the Ping-Pong table, was built for sleeping and sleeping only. It was overstuffed, vaguely gubernatorial. It smelled like the inside of a Lexus. Like something modern and medical and imperme-able that you could wipe the smell of death off easily, with a damp cloth, before the next person sat down to die in it.

The chair was the only major purchase Alfred ever made without Enid's approval. I see him at sixty-seven, a retired mechanical engineer walking the aisles of one of those mid-western furniture stores that only people who consider bargains immoral go to. I see him passing up lesser chairs—chairs with frivolous levers, chairs that don't seem important enough. For his entire working life he has taken naps in chairs subordinate to Enid's color schemes, and now he has received nearly five thousand dollars in retirement gifts. He has come to the store to spend the better part of this on a chair that celebrates, through its stature and costliness, the only activity in which he is truly himself. After a lifetime of providing for others, he needs even more than deep comfort and unlimited sleep: he needs public recognition of this need. Unfortunately, he fails to consider that monuments built for eternity are seldom comfortable for short-term accommodation. The chair he se-lects is outsized in the way of professional basketball shoes. I see his fingers trembling as they trace the multiple redun-dancy of the stitching. It's a lifetime chair—a mechanical engi-neer's chair, a chair designed to function under extraordinary stress, a chair with plenty of margin for error. On the minus side it's so much larger than any person who'd sit in it—is at once so yielding and so magnificent—that it forces its occupant into the postures of a sleeping child. In the coming years he won't settle into this chair so much as get lost in it.

When Alfred went to China to see Chinese mechanical engineers, Enid went along and the two of them visited a rug factory to buy a rug for their family room. They were still unaccustomed to spending money on themselves, and so they chose one of the least expensive rugs. It had a design from the *Book of Changes* in blue wool on a field of beige. The blue of the chair Alfred brought into the house a few years later vaguely matched the blue of the rug's design, and Enid, who was strict about matching, suffered the chair's arrival.

Soon, though, Alfred's hands began to spill decaffeinated coffee on the rug's beige expanses, and wild grandchildren from the Rocky Mountains left berries and crayons underfoot, and Enid began to feel that the rug was a mistake. It seemed to her that in trying to save money in life she had made many mistakes like this. She reached the point of thinking it would have been better to buy no rug than to buy this rug. Finally, as Alfred went to sleep in his chair, she grew bolder. Her own mother had left her a tiny inheritance years ago, and she had made certain investments. Interest had been added to principal, certain stocks had performed rather well, and now she had an income of her own. She reconceived the family room in greens and yellows. She ordered fabrics. A paperhanger came, and Alfred, who was napping temporarily in the dining room, leaped to his feet like a man with a bad dream.

"You're redecorating *again?*"

"It's my own money," Enid said. "This is how I'm spending it."

"And what about the money *I* spent? What about the work *I* did?"

This argument had been effective in the past—it was, you might say, the constitutional basis of the tyranny's legitimacy—but it didn't work now. "That rug is nearly ten years old, and we'll never get the coffee stains out," Enid answered.

Alfred gestured at his blue chair, which under the paper-hanger's plastic dropcloths looked like something you might deliver to a power station on a flatbed truck. He was trembling with incredulity, unable to believe that Enid could have forgotten this crushing refutation of her arguments, this over-whelming impediment to her plans; it was as if all the unfreedom and impossibility in which he'd spent his seven decades of life were embodied in this four-year-old but (because of its high quality) essentially brand-new chair. He was grinning, his face aglow with the awful perfection of his logic.

"And what about the chair, then?" he said. *"What about the chair?"*

Enid looked at the chair. Her expression was merely pained, no more. "I never liked that chair."

This was probably the most terrible thing she could have said to Alfred. The chair was the only sign he'd ever given of having a personal vision of the future. Enid's words filled him with such sorrow — he felt such pity for the chair, such solidarity with it, such astonished grief at its betrayal — that he pulled off the dropcloth and sank into its leather arms and fell asleep.

(This is one way of recognizing a place of enchantment: a suspiciously high incidence of narcolepsy.)

When it became clear that both the rug and Alfred's chair had to go, the rug was easily shed. Enid advertised in the free local paper and netted a nervous bird of a woman who was still making mistakes and whose fifties came out of her purse in a disorderly roll that she unpeeled and flattened with shaking fingers.

But the chair? The chair was a monument and a symbol and could not be parted from Alfred. It could only be relo-cated, and so it went into the basement and Alfred followed. And so in the house of the Lamberts, as in St. Jude, as in the country as a whole, life came to be lived underground.

•

Enid could hear him upstairs now, opening and closing drawers. In the streaklessly clean windows of the dining room was chaos. The berserk wind, the negating shadows. Now, of course, she had control of the upper floors. Now, when it was far too late.

Alfred stood in the master bedroom wondering why the drawers of his dresser were open, who had opened them, whether he had opened them himself. He could not help blaming Enid for his confusion. For witnessing it into existence. For existing, herself, as a person who could have opened these drawers.

"Al? What are you doing?"

He turned to the doorway where she'd appeared. He began a sentence: "I am —" but when he was taken by surprise, every sentence was an adventure in the woods; as soon as he could no longer see the light of the clearing from which he'd entered, it would come to him sickeningly that the crumbs he'd dropped for bearings had been eaten by birds, silent deft darting things that he couldn't quite see in the darkness but which were so numerous and swarming in their hunger that it seemed as if *they* were the darkness, as if the darkness weren't uniform, weren't an absence of light but a teeming and corpuscular thing, and indeed when as a studious teenager he'd encountered the word *crepuscular* in *McKay's Treasury of English Verse*, the corpuscles of biology had bled into his understanding of the word, so that for his entire adult life he'd seen in twilight a corpuscularity, as of the graininess of the high-speed film necessary for photography under conditions of low ambient light, as of a kind of sinister decay; and hence the panic of a man betrayed deep in the woods whose darkness was the darkness of starlings blotting out the sunset or black ants storming a dead opossum, a darkness that didn't just exist but actively *consumed* the bearings he had sensibly established for himself, lest he be lost; but in the instant of realizing he was lost, time became marvelously slow and he discovered hitherto unguessed eternities in the space between one word and the next, or rather he became trapped in that space between words and could only stand and watch as time sped on without him, the mindless part of him crashing on out of sight blindly through the woods while he, trapped, the grown-up Al, watched in considerable but oddly impersonal suspense to see if the panic-stricken little boy Freddie might, despite no longer knowing where he was or at what point he'd entered the woods of this sentence, still be fortunate enough to blunder into a clearing where Enid was waiting for him, unaware of any woods — "packing my suitcase," he heard himself say. This sounded right. Verb, possessive, noun. Here was a suitcase in front of him, an important confirmation. He'd betrayed nothing.

But Enid had spoken again. The audiologist had said he was mildly impaired. He frowned at her, not following.

"It's *Thursday*," she said, louder. "We're not going till *Saturday*."

"Saturday!" he echoed.

She berated him then, and for a while the crepuscular birds retreated, but outside the wind had blown the sun out, and it was getting very cold.

Two Poems by Jacqueline Osherow

Brief Encounter with a Hero, Name Unknown

It could have been a matter of modesty
It could have been the gold sewn in your dress
You might even have feared for your chastity
Maybe it was simple recklessness

Perhaps you couldn't part with that one dress,
Once rumpled by a skillful, knowing beau
Or were wearing it to hide a gaping abscess
Or were pregnant and ashamed to let it show

Maybe you'd seen a Western dubbed in Polish
Or Yiddish or Czech or whatever it was you spoke
And remembered some hokey John Wayne flourish
That downed four outlaws at a single stroke

Maybe you were an unexceptional girl
Who'd gone crazy on the claustrophobic ride
Maybe you had had a lover's quarrel
And, for days, been contemplating suicide

You could have been a fighter in the woods
And drilled this tactic over and over and over
Who knows? Perhaps you thought you'd beat the odds
Maybe it wasn't even the right maneuver

My father-in-law mentioned it in passing
When I asked how well he'd known his SS boss
(His job in Birkenau had been delousing;
They also used the zyklon-B for lice)

And he named one Schillinger, SS
And told how he had watched Schillinger die

When a new woman, ordered to undress
(You were going to the gas chamber, apparently)

Instead grabbed hold of Schillinger's own gun
And killed three other guards along with him
Such things, says my father-in-law, were common
(Needless to say, in seconds you had joined them)

It could have been a matter of modesty
It could have been the gold sewn in your dress
You might even have feared for your chastity
Maybe it was simple recklessness

On a City I Meant to Visit, Now at War

I heard tales of it on trains, from tireless travelers
And then its name would beckon from the drowsing hulls
Of steamers docked on Venice's back piers
Untroubled by the wild din of gulls.

I could so easily have boarded one
And seen what might have been the stuff of fables,
The spoutings of a circle of medieval whales
Turned, by shipwrecked sorcerers, to stone.

Then I'd have landed on a strange, bright shore
To climb a looming cliff side toward a tower
Whose ramparts seemed to touch the clouds' loose hem
And stare from the turret's jagged diadem

Through exes meant for crossbows in the solid walls
At fishing boats? swimmers? other steamers?
Or rumored clouds of islands linked by still canals
Whose waters dull the wistful coins of dreamers.

I might have watched, from the far-side, as the old-town square
Dispatched its slow procession toward a valley
And have seen some of these people, at least in miniature,
Whom we are giving up on almost daily

Or passed them near the marketplace's static clock,
Wiping idle kiosk counters clean
Or looking past the fortress at the trail of smoke
That says they've missed the steamer yet again

Or maybe I'd have gotten on a city bus,
Unfolded my impenetrable map,
And pointed to the museum looking helpless
When a fellow rider would have gotten up,

Gently led me off, taking my wrist,
To herd me on and off a string of trolley cars
And even come along to see the pictures
Like the man who did this once in Budapest

And kissed me on the mouth for quite some time.
Perhaps some years ago he left a bus
With a tourist from the now war-ravaged place
And rode beside her all her long way home

Where, stunned, he hardly knows which side he's on
And cannot lay his hands on any gun.
I wonder why I need his hazy face,
When I can hear, as well as anyone, this teacher's voice,

Saying, on the radio, that she'll starve to death
If she isn't first flattened by a bomb
That is, until my kettle's mounting steam
Interrupts her with a sudden surge of breath.

Is it heartlessness or just modern science
That enables me to make a cup of tea

While she, just as calm, foretells her death to me?
She deserves, at the very least, perfect silence.

But there's always some noise — a wind, a car,
A household's share of reassuring hums;
I can't invoke pure silence any more
Than I can picture cliffs and palaces and falling bombs,

Which is, let's be honest, what's required here
And I can't even see the cliffs and palaces,
Only jumbled hillsides, roofs and cornices
Borrowed from the cities that I've seen before

And the steamers bobbing near the Grand Canal,
The Hungarian leaving me a last kiss on the cheek,
And in answer to my question *the most beautiful?*
A woman on a train saying *Dubrovnik*

James Longenbach

Things You'll Never Know

I was so young that I invented loss,
The image of the mother's face receding
On the far edge of the broken bed,

A child's face, implacable, returning
To a fountain in a foreign city—
Gods and tritons cracked and thin

Behind a chain-link fence that blurred
Into a veil, like the one that draws us,
Following ourselves, into the past.

Not even Rome is consolation for the death
Of children and to think about the future
Is to think of children and to think

About a child is to think of death,
If only since the child is the part of us
That's disappeared: Aeneas, having mixed

The ashes with the wine, surveying all
The future generations' gifts to Rome,
Attends to one tall youth, more beautiful

Than any other but with clouded brows
And downcast eyes, the child we will mourn,
For whom the lilies offer nothing in return.

It would be useful to believe we'd meet
Again, and all of Christianity
Seems poised against its knowledge

That the one who dies is not the mother
But the child, Jesus railing at heaven
And the sky, unanswering, omnipotent,

The image of what every parent feels
In the face of suffering that nothing
We have learned to do throughout the long

And unrewarded climb into adulthood
Can assuage. The possibilities
Are burdensome enough to think of

Much less see: the snowplow sliding off
The exit ramp or blond hair mimicking
A breezy summer at the bottom of the pool.

We're children then ourselves, incapable
Of action or intelligible speech —
A drooling infant sucking on his hands

Like Ugolino, who must hear his children
Whimpering for bread and bear their charity —
Our pain will lessen, father, if you eat us —

And do nothing but observe the sunlight
Leaking through the grille as one by one
The children dwindle to the floor and die.

These stories can't be told, as Dante says,
By tongues that babble in a language
Capable of words like *mom* and *dad*.

Our language is the child's world
And when we speak, no matter what we say,
We're longing for a world we've lost forever,

Only to find out, if we begin to poke
Around the dingy corners of the mind,
That it's a world we never could have had.

Some people think they have an easy access
To whatever made them what they are,
And you can watch them, raising children,

As they replicate each long-lost pleasure
For themselves, pancakes wide
As dinner plates, served up with confidence

That what worked once may, recreated,
Work again. These are the parents
Who won't pay the piper once he's rid

The town of rats—the children lost,
Abandoned, past all help, all hurting,
Who will follow him into the hills

Across rat river, where the ghosts of children
Never born will whisper *play with me*—
And we awaken in a sweat and wander

Down the frozen corridor to check
Their beds, their breathing, too embarrassed
To admit that when we dream about their deaths

We want to die. For if the pancakes work—
Piano lessons, weekends at the barn—
The children take the place of loss,

The part that's dead, and no one, having put
The past to sleep, however nurturing,
However fondly we remember it,

Could want to see its specter wandering
That hallway in the middle of the night
To ask for water or to say *I'm cold*.

The truth of childhood is theater,
An empty bed, our own breath faltering,
As when the old man who refused to grieve

Before the mangled body of his son
Admits that he has acted like a boy
Who plays a grown-up part, *speaks burly words*

But when he thinks upon his infant weakness
Is transformed into a child. We play
The roles long before we comprehend them,

But the comprehension only comes
When we admit we'll never understand
The world as we imagined grown-ups might.

The truth of theater is child's play,
A company of boys who take the stage
Pretending they're exactly what they are.

We need to hear these stories and rehearse
The possibilities, as if pure love
Were difficult to see, as if we'd rather

See the body dead than trusting its desires,
Boys afraid of their own loveliness,
A dingy room, the mutilated trees.

We wander through the underbrush,
Survey the bottles and the rusted cans,
And, finding nothing, are confirmed

In the suspicion that we need to lose—
Lose furniture, the books, our clothes,
And all of the generic memories that from

The moment of our birth have worked their way
Beneath the skin—that over time will burst
Like capillaries on our hands and thighs,

A signal to remind us of the world
That we've internalized and can't abandon
Since in losing it, we lose ourselves.

The body cannot tolerate an emptiness,
And as the wound begins to swell, our grief
Replaces what we've lost, grows vast,

Until the grieving seems ridiculous,
Which is the only thing that grief could be.
The notion of the loss, a fantasy,

Can be enough to open wide the sutures
Of an ordinary day, as when a child
Walks the dog alone, and far above

The traffic and the melting slush,
Although we recognize she had to go,
A panic fills the space she left behind.

You are as fond of grief as of your child,
Says a voice inside us, harsh, uncompromising
As the murky sidewalk down below.

But we retaliate, and like the mother
Who begins to grieve before the prince
Is gone, we play a scene, put on a show:

Grief fills the room up of my absent child,
Lies in his bed, walks up and down with me,
And stuffs his vacant garments with his form.

My child plays ferociously with things
We've given her and things she's found
And things she'll never know. I'm not too old

To play along. Before she spoke
I thought I'd come to know her perfectly—
That just by listening, I'd have an answer

For whatever wakes her in the middle
Of the night. But parents have
No special purview on the human heart

And cannot know their children any better
Than they comprehend themselves.
There's one more thing. We tossed

Some lire in the empty pool, and as if
Parched stone could hear us, water burst
From every orifice, the past undone,

And wonder rising through the air like mist.
I don't remember what we wished,
But anything that ever found us was you.

Eric Pankey

A Basket of Apricots

Flustered (words always made him flustered),
He thought of saying never mind, but instead
Changed the subject. She, the listener, listened

As he turned away from his confession.
She wondered why he should feel so ill at ease
Describing, now, a basket of apricots

That had been set down in the square of sunlight
Between them. How he went on: *blush*, *fragrant suede*,
Declivity, *the hidden burled pit*, . . . !

All of it seemed overwrought and wrong to her.
Angry, she thought him a fool. And he, too,
Grew angry and said, You never listen.

To what, she said, What are you saying to me?
By then she could not look at him. She watched
The smudges of gnats hover above the fruit.

Next, he might call the sunlight *gold lamé*.
Next—who knows what he might say next, and worse,
She thought, what he means? Then, when he mentioned

The sunlight, which she had to admit
Was lustrous and at this point a way to change
The subject, she laughed, willing to forgive.

But that laugh pricked him and he said, Never mind.
What he had first meant to say now seemed so clear
That he felt like blurting it out. There, he'd say.

But however he phrased it to himself,
Imagining her as the listener,
It seemed hardly worth saying. There? she'd say back,

As if to throw out the evidence he'd entered.
The gnats, buoyed on the too-sweet air, brought to mind
Lines from Shakespeare he thought to recite:

"Who can . . . / Cloy the hungry edge of appetite
By bare imagination of a feast?"
For both their sakes he thought the better of it.

And when she lifted her hand from her lap, he hoped
She would reach across the table to hold his hand.
But she slapped at the air and shooed away the gnats.

Three Poems by Paul Kane

Concedo Nulli

In Anderlecht, the Maison d'Erasme
sits in an elegant courtyard as if
withdrawn from the vulgar world — *concedo
nulli* read the signet rings in hot wax.
Across the way, l'Église de Saint-Pierre
crumbles in disrepair, its scaffolding
empty, all work halted. The foundations,
undermined by traffic and time, subsist.
Through a side door I step inside just as
the choir begins afternoon practice.
Schoolchildren, instructed by the priest, sit
on wooden chairs in the nave. One boy walks
in late, apologetic, takes his place.
They sing a Latin Erasmus would have
smiled at, weakly. The church is cold, colder
than outside. It is entirely local,
while the Maison functions as a locale.
The humanist never left the Church, from
which he was always apart: wit, satire,
ridicule — even mortared stone can rot.
In the faltering voices rehearsing
the hymns, there is no irony — and if
the priest takes pleasure in the sound, as do
I seated by a pillar in shadows,
it is because for moments at a time
what's praised is neither knowledge nor folly,
but an absence we cannot account for.

Framing

Toenail, bracket, header, joist and brace —
words nailed into place

in the grammar of the addition.
It all adds up, as each edition

of the plan is issued daily
over morning coffee. Rarely

does our thinking match what yesterday
came clear as the day

before. This protean porch has gone
from screen to glass along

the imagined way to its present form:
all open air, framed in two-by-fours

through which sky and field
are ordered by words that yield

structure and a sense of place:
toenail, bracket, header, joist and brace.

The Repentant Magdalen

after Georges de La Tour

We are hollowed out by death, as by life.
How many moments to balance the weight
of forgetfulness — that knowingness which
is fear of an unknowing, a darkness?

You stare at the image of your image
until the glass reflects back the room where
you sit, in judgement, in the wavering
light, looking for the life within the skull.

Your fingers probe the sockets, your lips taste
the salt of your own flesh: you are not what
you seem—or, what you seem is what you are,
but that is a penance the future holds.

The room darkens, a trick of light suspends
the painting as an image in the air.
Who now comtemplates? To whom attribute
these dense tribulations, this self-flaring?

You—parabolic!—who exist beside
me here, touch the radiant cell of this
life, illumine me beyond reflection,
and make remorse the glass of what I am.

Two Poems by Serena J. Fox

Power not Peace

shit flows downhill he who loves power
gets to be king he who loves love
gets to be priest kings and priests
resurrect absolutes deny existence

of excrement and orifice suffering
is proof worship is suffering he who
suffers shit will not have power
he may have peace peace is indifference

to power and love Mr. Squillante at peace
stacks his meal tray with turds smears
his roommate with feces a man wakes
anointed screams and arrests during

the "code" Mr. Squillante dubs feces
on walls and himself Mr. Squillante is
neither king nor priest he does not
know what he is doing.

The Angio

My father lies at the end of my white coat,
witnessing his own angiography. He jokes,
winces occasionally. The techs are reading
Malcolm X. Two vein grafts are

occluded. The internal mammary artery graft
looks good in many different projections. In
this decade, we are redirected towards the
mammary, for our hearts' blood. It

strikes me that my father has no grandchildren.
A patient of mine had his coronaries done for the
third time with a graft from his gastric artery.
Truly, the way to a man's heart . . .

ha, ha . . . We have bitten of the heart and the
heart is The Tree. The serpent recoils postop.
Not one of us is ready for the next exposure.
I did not want to

bring him here, because I did not want him to
know how easily he fits into my pocket, and
to what lengths I'll go to keep him there. My
father observed the

autopsy of his father, who walked around Miami
for a week with a massive coronary occlusion,
and he can — my fingers at his temples,
holding all I ever need

to be — watch steadily as the
dye, serpentine, drips
down the screen.

Two Poems by Phillip Sterling

Pedestrian Tunnel to Clinch Park Zoo, Winter 1964

Not the kiss alone
    but an essence of kiss,
its dark matter left undisclosed
by heavily clothed and insulated
bodies, the lips
    alone reckoning detail:

a questionable touch,
    the muffle of traffic and
slush, and the shy heart racing
across weakened ice disappears
like a snowmobile
    into depths of West Bay.

Only at memory's thaw
    will loss be found, paler,
older, though not so cold,
remarkably life-like, nudging
the impossible
    shore or loitering

against the snow fence
    near the entrance barred
for the season, hesitant at first,
then willing, even anxious,
to risk in awkward light
    a witnessed kiss.

Mechanical Failure

I'd just then turned away
from recording all the charge slips I'd laid
aside during morning rush—gas sales,
mostly, some doughnuts, coffee—
making up for the time I'd used
to refresh pots or fool

with cup dispensers, which
jam up fairly regular, most often
when traffic's tight—and since no car had
pulled in for a while, I thought
I'd get a break and maybe smoke
out back—that's when I heard

the awful wail of brakes,
the burning screech, and turning back around
I saw a brilliant blue Freightliner
run the intersection like
there's no tomorrow, jump the curb
and bear down for the pumps.

Oh my God! I thought. There's
nothing between me and *up in flames* but
glass and counterspace—the register,
one cellophane-wrapped yellow
rose, and a half-full plastic tub
of 5-cent bubble gum.

So what was I *supposed*
to think? I knew a woman once who'd lost
a child at birth—she said she'd never
be the same. And I knew then
if I survived, if for some saint's
mad purpose I was spared,

I'd feel such letdowns too—
at every high-pitched squeal, every kitten
mew, every desperate metallic squawk—
and sure enough the truck just
grazed the number seven pump, stopped
short of snapping one and

five like matches. A sharp
smell of petroleum made my sore eyes
sear. You know, I left that job for good
that afternoon, and now I
just sell Avon on the side. I
guess I'll see my birthday

after all—no one is
forty-three very long. And you know,
the driver said that, bursting through
the door: "The whole works just up
and quit approaching forty-four!"
He'd been quite shaken too.

Sign Collection

Frayed strings of geese
~~yap~~ over south this
~~blue cloud~~ afternoon
when nearly

every day/~~has~~ left October:
~~not~~ long now
till the colors,
snuggled under, sum up white:
then, we'll ~~walk into the~~
~~wind to first~~ black
streaks ~~to~~ trunk and post,
downwind standings,

because among the turnings
is the winter we won't
find our way from or to;
~~too~~ cold, just cold.

the cold, meanwhile, just cold.

A manuscript page from the poem "Sign Collection" by A.R. Ammons.

A.R. Ammons

The Art of Poetry LXXIII

*One day in the winter of 1987 Archie Ammons was driving
north on the I-95 in Florida when a gigantic hill of rubble*

*came into view. The sight sparked an epiphany: "I thought
maybe that was the sacred image of our time," the poet said.
Upon his return to Ithaca, New York, where he is the Goldwin
Smith Professor of Poetry at Cornell University, Ammons tried
to write a long poem entitled* Garbage. *Nothing came of the
first attempt. Two years later, however, the image returned
and wouldn't let him off so easily. He wrote the poem quickly,
finished it in a season, then put it aside. A major medical
predicament—a massive coronary in August 1989 and triple
bypass surgery a year later—intervened. When Ammons returned to the poem, he was no longer sure of it, and when
it was accepted by his publisher, he was surprised. Nobody
else was when this extraordinary work went on to win the 1993
National Book Award in poetry, the second time Ammons
has been so honored. Ammons received the Frost Medal from
the Poetry Society of America in April 1994. Later that year,
he and his wife, Phyllis, drove to Washington (the Ammonses
do not believe in flying) to collect the Bobbitt Prize, which
sounds like something a Court TV reporter made up but is
actually an accolade bestowed by the Library of Congress.*

*Born in Whiteville, North Carolina, in 1926—"big, jaun-
diced and ugly," in his words—Archie Randolph Ammons
grew up on a family tobacco farm during the meanest years
of the Great Depression. He had two sisters; one brother died
as an infant, a loss mourned in his powerful poem "Easter
Morning." The hymns Archie heard every Sunday in church
had their mostly unconscious influence on his poetry, which
he began writing in the navy during World War II. Some of
his first efforts were comic poems about shipmates aboard
the destroyer escort on which he served in the South Pacific.
Ammons recently wrote the poem "Ping Jockeys" when he
found out that two pillars of the New York School of poets,
James Schuyler and Frank O'Hara, had also been trained as
sonar men on Key West, where Ammons learned "how to lay
down depth-charge patterns on enemy hulks."*

*Ammons got out of the navy in 1946. He was able to attend
college thanks to that piece of enlightened social legislation,
the G.I. Bill, which paid his way at Wake Forest College,*

"The Paris Review remains the single most important little magazine this country has produced."

—T. Coraghessan Boyle

THE
PARIS
REVIEW

Enclosed is my check for:

☐ $34 for 1 year (4 issues)

(All payment must be in U.S. funds. Postal surcharge of $10 per 4 issues outside USA)

☐ Send me information on becoming a *Paris Review* Associate.

Bill this to my Visa/MasterCard:

Sender's full name and address needed for processing credit cards.

_____
Card number   Exp. date

☐ New subscription ☐ Renewal subscription
☐ New address

Name _____

Address _____

City _____ State _____ Zip code _____

Please send gift subscription to:

Name _____

Address _____

City _____ State _____ Zip code _____

Gift announcement signature _____

call (718)539-7085

Please send me the following:

☐ The Paris Review T-Shirt ($15.00)
   Color _____ Size _____ Quantity _____
☐ The following back issues: Nos. _____

   See listing at back of book for availability.

Name _____

Address _____

City _____ State _____ Zip code _____

☐ Enclosed is my check for $ _____
☐ Bill this to my Visa/MasterCard:

_____
Card number   Exp. date

BUSINESS REPLY MAIL

FIRST CLASS   PERMIT NO. 3119   FLUSHING, N.Y.

POSTAGE WILL BE PAID BY ADDRESSEE

THE PARIS REVIEW
45-39 171 Place
FLUSHING NY   11358-9892

BUSINESS REPLY MAIL

FIRST CLASS   PERMIT NO. 3119   FLUSHING, N.Y.

POSTAGE WILL BE PAID BY ADDRESSEE

THE PARIS REVIEW
45-39 171 Place
FLUSHING NY   11358-9892

where he began as a premed student. In a writing class taught
by E.E. Folk, he learned his method of "the transforming
idea"—how to organize materials gathered from disparate
sources—which he has continued to use in his poems. Another
course with a decisive impact on Ammons's life was intermedi-
ate Spanish, which was taught by Phyllis Plumbo, a recent
graduate of Douglass College, then the women's division of
Rutgers University. Archie walked her home one day, and
the couple will soon celebrate their forty-seventh wedding
anniversary.

Ammons did not enter the academic life until he was close to
forty. In 1949, he became the principal of the tiny elementary
school in the island village of Cape Hatteras. For most of the
next decade he worked as a sales executive in his father-in-law's
biological glass company on the southern New Jersey shore.
Ammons published Ommateum, *his first book of poems, with*
Dorrance, a vanity press, in 1955; a mere sixteen copies were
sold in the next five years. (A copy today would fetch two
thousand dollars.) He joined the Cornell University faculty
in 1964 and has taught there ever since.

Expressions of Sea Level, *Ammons's second collection, came*
out in 1964 from Ohio State University Press and triggered
the most prolific period in his career. He went rapidly from
total obscurity to wide acclaim. His prematurely entitled Collected Poems 1951-1971 *won the National Book Award in*
1973. He won the coveted Bollingen Prize for his long poem
Sphere (1974), *in which the governing image was the earth*
as photographed from outer space. Ammons's method for
writing a long poem is, in a nutshell, finding "a single image
that can sustain multiplicity."

For a poet who believes in inspiration and spontaneity, Am-
mons is a creature of fixed habit. He begins his days having
coffee in the Temple of Zeus, a coffee bar on the Cornell
campus, with a handful of chums such as the Nobel Prize-
winning chemist and poet Roald Hoffmann. (Hoffmann, who
has written three books of poems, unabashedly calls Ammons
his guru.) Archie professes to despise the poetry writing indus-
try and has a skeptical attitude on the whole question of

whether poetry can be taught. Yet his own reputation among students past and present is high. A casual exchange of poems with Archie can turn into a memorable experience. "I have coffee sometimes in the morning for years with people," Ammons says. "And then it may be five or ten years afterwards they will show me something they've written and I will suddenly feel that I know them better in that minute than I have known them through all the conversations that had taken place before."

This interview was conducted by a variety of means. We began with two long sessions with a tape recorder in Ammons's house in Ithaca. Briefer exchanges in person, on the phone and by mail followed at regular intervals. It was as if we were continuing a conversation that had begun in 1976, when we met, and of which this interview is a sample and a distillation. We shelved it for a while while we worked together on The Best American Poetry 1994, *for which Archie made the selections, and then we picked up where we had left off.*

Ammons's twenty-third book of poems, Brink Road, *was published by Norton in the spring of 1996.* Set in Motion, *a gathering of his prose, will appear in the Poets on Poetry Series of the University of Michigan Press.*

A.R. AMMONS

Aren't you going to start with the typical *Paris Review* interview question, such as, "What do you write with or on?"

INTERVIEWER

All right. [*Pause*] What do you write with or on?

AMMONS

My poems begin on the typewriter. If I'm home—and I rarely write anything elsewhere—I write on an Underwood standard upright, manual, not electric, which I bought used in Berkeley in 1951 or 1952. It had been broken and was rewelded. It's worked without almost any attention for forty-four years. When I was away a few times, for a year or a summer, I wrote on similar typewriters. It's hard now to find regular typewriter paper (as opposed to Xerox paper) and ribbons.

I sometimes scribble words or phrases or poems with a pen and pencil if I'm traveling or at work. But I like the typewriter because it allows me to set up the shapes and control the space. Though I don't care for much formality (in fact, I hate ceremony), I need to lend a formal cast, at least, to the motions I so much love.

INTERVIEWER

When you begin a poem, do you have a specific source of inspiration, or do you start with words and push them around the page until they begin to take shape?

AMMONS

John Ashbery says that he would never begin to write a poem under the force of inspiration or with an idea already given. He prefers to wait until he has absolutely nothing to say, and then begins to find words and to sort them out and to associate with them. He likes to have the poem occur on the occasion of its occurrence rather than to be the result of some inspiration or imposition from the outside. Now I think that's a brilliant point of view. That's not the way I work. I've always been highly energized and have written poems in spurts. From the god-given first line right through the poem. And I don't write two or three lines and then come back the next day and write two or three more; I write the whole poem at one sitting and then come back to it from time to time over the months or years and rework it.

INTERVIEWER

Did you write, say, "The City Limits" in one sitting?

AMMONS

Absolutely.

INTERVIEWER

The eighteen lines of that poem do seem to be a single outcry. Were there changes after you wrote it?

AMMONS

Hardly a one. I sent the poem to Harold Bloom, something I almost never had done, and he admired it and sent a note to me not to change a word.

INTERVIEWER

Bloom has been a longtime champion of your work. How long have you known him?

AMMONS

He was here for the year in 1968, and his children were the same age as my son John, and they became playmates. Harold and I became friends. I didn't regularly send him my poems, and he never suggested how they be written. But I wrote "The City Limits" and I wanted to share it with him. It was not literary business. It was friendship business. That was in 1971.

INTERVIEWER

Does inspiration originate in nature, in external reality, or in the self?

AMMONS

I think it comes from anxiety. That is to say, either the mind or the body is already rather highly charged and in need of some kind of expression, some way to crystallize and relieve the pressure. And it seems to me that if you're in that condition and an idea, an insight, an association occurs to you, then that energy is released through the expression of that insight or idea, and after the poem is written, you feel a certain resolution and calmness. Well, I won't say a "momentary stay against confusion" (Robert Frost's phrase) but that's what I mean. I think it comes from that. You know, Bloom says somewhere that poetry *is* anxiety.

INTERVIEWER

Bloom talks about the anxiety of influence, but you talk about the influence of anxiety.

AMMONS

Absolutely. The invention of a poem frequently is how to find a way to resolve the complications that you've gotten yourself into. I have a little poem about this that says that the poem begins as life does, takes on complications as novels do, and at some point stops. Something has to be invented before you can work your way out of it, and that's what happens at the very center of a poem.

INTERVIEWER

What poem are you referring to?

AMMONS

It's called "The Swan Ritual." It's in the *Collected Poems*.

INTERVIEWER

I have this picture of you taking long walks along places mentioned in your poems, such as Cascadilla Falls here in Ithaca or Corsons Inlet on the New Jersey shore, and writing as you were walking, writing out something longhand.

AMMONS

Or memorizing it in your head.

INTERVIEWER

Did you do that?

AMMONS

Yes, oh yes. Not something as long as "Corsons Inlet," but shorter poems. I've done that here in Ithaca and down there many times.

INTERVIEWER

"Corsons Inlet" is 128 lines long. Did you write it at the end of the long walk described in the poem?

AMMONS

Yes, and at one sitting.

INTERVIEWER

A poet of inspiration, a poet who depends on inspiration, isn't likely to write on schedule, and I don't suppose you do.

AMMONS

No, I never sit down or stand up to try to write. It's like trying to go to the bathroom when you feel no urge. Unless I have something already moving through the mind, I don't go to the typewriter at all. The world has so many poems in it, it has never seemed to me very smart to force one more upon the world. If there isn't one there to write, you just leave it alone.

INTERVIEWER

Why do you write?

AMMONS

I write for love, respect, money, fame, honor, redemption. I write to be included in a world I feel rejected by. But I don't want to be included by surrendering myself to expectations. I want to buy my admission to others by engaging their interests and feelings, doing the least possible damage to my feelings and interests but changing theirs a bit. I think I was not aware early on of those things. I wrote early on because it was there to do and because if anything good happened in the poem I felt good. Poems are experiences as well as whatever else they are, and for me now, nothing, not respect, honor, money, seems as supportive as just having produced a body of work, which I hope is, all considered, good.

INTERVIEWER

It took you a long time to get respect, honor, money and fame for your work. You had the support of Josephine Miles when you were a graduate student at Berkeley, and you had poems accepted by *Poetry* magazine in the 1950s. But you had very few readers, and you weren't winning a lot of prizes and grants.

AMMONS

That's right. I spent twenty years writing on my own without any recognition. You know, I started writing in 1945. In 1955 I published a book of my own with a vanity publisher, my first book, *Ommateum*. It wasn't until 1964 that I had a book accepted by Ohio State University Press, *Expressions of Sea Level*.

INTERVIEWER

And the quality of that work, when looked at now?

AMMONS

Well, it's the best I have. It still sustains my reputation.

INTERVIEWER

So you found it possible to be a poet, and to thrive as a poet, without the material trappings of celebration and success.

AMMONS

I couldn't avoid being a poet. I was really having a pretty rough time of things, and I had a lot of energy, and poems were practically the only recourse I had to alleviate that energy and that anxiety. I take no credit for all the poems I've written. They were a way of releasing anxiety.

INTERVIEWER

When you say you were having a rough time, do you mean financially?

AMMONS

I had really no clear-cut direction to my life for those years.
I was working in business, not necessarily getting anywhere.
It was just a lack of definition and direction. Financially, I
didn't have a great deal of money, but I wasn't impoverished
at that time.

INTERVIEWER

You grew up impoverished in North Carolina.

AMMONS

We grew up rather poor, yes. But we didn't think of ourselves as poor. You've heard this said many times, I'm sure,
about people in the depression. We had a farm. It had been
created as a sustenance farm, that is, you grew as many things
as you might possibly need. My two sisters and I — I had two
brothers but they died young — were never hungry. We always
had clothes to wear. There was no money, however, in the
South. I mean, during the depression, there were actually no
coins. People bartered. We had no money, so we were poor
in that sense, but my family, in Southern terms, was fairly
distinguished. My uncle was sheriff of the county for eight
consecutive terms, longer than anyone had been. It was a
highly prestigious job in those days, and he was a splendid
working man who was always erect and never carried a gun.
He had a reputation for going into the most dangerous places
unarmed and telling murderers or suspected murderers to
come with him, and they would do it. He was also a considerable landowner in the county and owned what later became
a whole beach down at the ocean, which was about forty miles
from us. So he was a wealthy man and a highly prestigious
man. I honored him greatly as a child. He sometimes helped
us in the winters when we were broke.

So I was caught in the contradiction of feeling that I came
from a good line and yet being inhibited as far as resources
went. Since I was the only surviving Ammons of an enormous
family, I was frequently told I was going to inherit forests and

farms and things like that. But I didn't. By the time my uncle
passed away I had left that region and never went back.

INTERVIEWER

Sometimes it seems that the economic circumstances of one's
childhood do play a determining role in one's psychological
makeup later on. You can never really transcend those early
insecurities.

AMMONS

I agree. Though there were other insecurities in my youth:
the death of the two brothers, for example.

INTERVIEWER

Were they younger brothers?

AMMONS

Yes. I was four when the brother eighteen months old died.
I still carry images of that whole thing. And then the last
member of our family was born dead. So I was the only son
left.

INTERVIEWER

Did you like working on the farm?

AMMONS

I hated it. You had to work in all kinds of weather. In the
winter, you were in the swamp cutting trees for the fuel you
needed in the summer for curing the tobacco. I mean it was
just a constant round of hard work without reward because
we remained in debt year after year after year.

INTERVIEWER

Did you read books at home?

AMMONS

That came later. The only book I can remember having in
the house apart from textbooks was the first eleven pages of

Robinson Crusoe. I read that so many times I practically had it by memory. I don't know where the eleven pages came from, but there they were. Otherwise we read the Bible in Sunday school and we sang hymns. That was my exposure to words. And, by the way, I think that hymns have had an enormous influence on what I've written because they're the words I first heard and memorized.

INTERVIEWER

When did you start writing?

AMMONS

When I went to high school (which in those times included the eighth grade) I wrote an essay, and the teacher praised it highly and told all our classes, even the senior classes, about it. So I began to get some encouragement pretty early on about writing.

INTERVIEWER

What was the essay about?

AMMONS

We were asked to read articles in *Reader's Digest* and then to write our own version of the substance. I wrote about a cow they were trying to breed that would be only about thirty inches high but would give vast amounts of milk. I must have done this in an excellent style because as you can see the subject matter is not all that thrilling.

INTERVIEWER

You mentioned Sunday school hymns as an important influence. I can see that in your very first poems, your "I am Ezra" poems. Certainly the religious impulse — the resolve to render the sacred in terms of the secular, to wed the lowly and the divine — is in much of your work. In a poem as recent as "The Damned" a mountaineer surrounded by silent peaks looks down from the summit and supposes that "these damned came of being / near the sanctified, wherever one finds / one one finds the other." Were you brought up to be serious about religion?

AMMONS

My mother was Methodist, but there was no Methodist church in our rural community, so I never went to a Methodist service. My father was Baptist. The New Hope Baptist Church was two miles away next to the elementary school. Nearer to us, less than a mile away, was the Spring Branch Fire-Baptized Pentecostal Church. I went to Sunday school there and the family sometimes attended preaching on Sundays, prayer meetings on Wednesday nights or occasional weekly revivals. Once a two-week course in reading music was offered there — the do-re-me-so method — and I attended that when I was about eleven or twelve. As for the Baptist church, I went there for the Christmas Eve celebrations. For some reason, a paper bag containing an orange and apple, raisins and a few English walnuts or pecans was always under the tree for me. The funerals in my family took place at the Baptist church. My little brothers, my grandmother, my aunts and uncles, and my father and mother were buried there. The Baptist Church represented a higher social and intellectual class than did the Pentecostal. I identify coldly with the family religion. I take my religious spirit, whatever that is, from the Fire-Baptized Pentecostal.

INTERVIEWER

Reading your poems I sometimes feel that they employ scientific means to reach a kind of religious end. I suppose I've always taken it for granted that you stopped going to church and that at some point — perhaps in your days as a sonar man in the navy during World War II — poetry became the means by which you expressed your religious convictions.

AMMONS

One day, when I was nineteen, I was sitting on the bow of the ship anchored in a bay in the South Pacific. As I looked at the land, heard the roosters crowing, saw the thatched huts, et cetera, I thought down to the water level and then to the immediately changed and strange world below the waterline. But it was the line inscribed across the variable landmass, determining where people would or would not live, where palm trees would or could not grow, that hypnotized me. The whole world changed as a result of an interior illumination: the water level was not what it was because of a single command by a higher power but because of an average result of a host of actions — runoff, wind currents, melting glaciers. I began to apprehend things in the dynamics of themselves — motions and bodies — the full account of how we came to be a mystery with still plenty of room for religion, though, in my case, a religion of what we don't yet know rather than what we are certain of. I was de-denominated.

INTERVIEWER

When did you join the navy?

AMMONS

I think it was 1944. I came out in 1946. I was in for nineteen months, about twelve of them in the South Pacific on a destroyer escort. It was on board this ship that I found an anthology of poetry in paperback. And I began to imitate those poems then, and I wrote from then on.

INTERVIEWER

Did you write about home and America and North Carolina or about what was happening in the South Pacific?

AMMONS

Mostly about what was happening in the South Pacific, including some humorous poems about the other members of the crew.

INTERVIEWER

What has happened to these poems?

AMMONS

Oh, they're around.

INTERVIEWER

Did you continue writing poems in civilian life?

AMMONS

I had never stopped writing but after having gotten a degree, the B.S. in general science at Wake Forest, I borrowed the money to go back for a summer of education courses and then taught the first year as the principal of a three-teacher school in Cape Hatteras. That was 1949-1950. That same fall, 1949, I got married. My wife, Phyllis, had been to Berkeley and liked it. So after a year of teaching, we went to Berkeley for two years. And there I did a good many English courses, completing the undergraduate degree. I had minored in English at Wake Forest so I completed that degree and did almost all the work toward a master's. And then we left and came back to south Jersey. I lived there for twelve years before coming here to Ithaca.

INTERVIEWER

I know that you worked in your father-in-law's biological glass factory as a vice president in charge of sales. Were you interested in the work or was it dull?

AMMONS

It wasn't dull. I have a poem somewhere explaining how running a business is like writing a poem. In business, for example, you bring in the raw materials and then subject them to a certain kind of human change. You introduce the raw materials into a system of order, like the making of a poem, and once the matter is shaped it's ready to be shipped. I mean, the incoming and outgoing energies have achieved a kind of balance. Believe it or not, I felt completely confident in the work I was doing. And did it, I think, well.

INTERVIEWER

That raises an interesting question. Most American poets work in universities and many if not most were trained in creative writing programs. It's the rare exception who makes his or her living outside the academy, as you did. I'm not entirely convinced that this academic dependence is a healthy state of affairs.

AMMONS

Me neither. In my own case, working in industry wasn't exhausting — I mean poetically exhausting. I could write all the time. It's been true for me that, in the thirty years I've been teaching, my writing is done before the semester starts. The time I do any writing is Christmas vacation. That's when I wrote "Hibernaculum" and *Tape* and the "Essay on Poetics." Most of the things have been done between semesters or during the summers.

INTERVIEWER

When were you invited to teach at Cornell?

AMMONS

I received an invitation from David Ray to give a reading here. He'd seen poems of mine in *The Hudson Review*. Also, I had that same year relieved Denise Levertov for six months as poetry editor of *The Nation*. And I had, without knowing the man, accepted a poem by David Ray and published it. I suppose as a kind of return gesture, he invited me to come give a reading for $50 at Cornell, and then he saw my poems in *The Hudson Review* and raised the fee to $150. So I came in July of 1963 and gave the reading and afterwards James McConkey and Baxter Hathaway and others asked me if I would be interested in teaching. And though I was not a teacher and had not taught, I said yes, because my wife and I were ready to make a move, and so we came to Cornell.

INTERVIEWER

And you've been here ever since.

AMMONS

They were very good to me. At first I was the only non-Ph.D. in the English department, and they welcomed me and kept me. They gave me tenure. I thought it was quite remarkable.

INTERVIEWER

Your standing-room-only poetry reading in Ithaca last December was memorable. I never thought I'd see you in a tuxedo. Did the event change your feelings about poetry readings, or confirm them? Why do you suppose people go to readings anyway?

AMMONS

It's a great mystery. When you consider how boring and painful nearly all poetry readings are, it's a wonder anyone shows up. And, wisely, few people do. I think it's not a love of poetry readings that attracts those who do come but theater: to see what the beast, possibly already heard of, looks like in person; to make a poetry-business connection that could prove useful; to see who else comes to poetry readings; to endure pain and purgation; to pass one's books or pamphlets on to the reader; to see the reader mess up, suffer, lose control, and to enjoy the remarkable refreshment of finding him no less human, vulnerable or fallible, than oneself.

INTERVIEWER

It may be time for another official *Paris Review* interview question: what advice do you give to young writers?

AMMONS

First of all, I omit praising them too much if I think that will be the catalyst that causes them to move into a seizure with a poetic way of life. Because I know how difficult that can be, and I tend to agree with Rilke that if it's possible for you to live some other life, by all means do so. If it seems to me that the person can't live otherwise than as a writer of poetry, then I encourage them to go ahead and do it. However,

the advice splits, depending on how I feel about the person.
If I think he's really a genuine poet, I'd like to encourage him
to get out into the so-called real world. If he seems like a poet
who's going to get by through a kind of pressure of having
to turn in so many poems per week in order to get a good
grade or having to publish a book of poems in order to get
promoted, then I encourage him to go to an M.F.A program
somewhere and become a so-called professional poet. You get
to know people who know how to publish books, you begin
to advance your career. I don't think that has very much to do
with *real* poetry. It sometimes happens that these professional
M.F.A. people are also poets; but it *rarely* happens.

INTERVIEWER

You once said that trying to make a living from poetry is
like putting chains on butterfly wings.

AMMONS

Right. I'd stand by that.

INTERVIEWER

How do you feel about government support of the arts?

AMMONS

I detest it. I detest it on many grounds, but three first. And
the first is that the government gouges money from people
who may need it for other purposes. Second, the money forced
from needy average citizens is then filtered through the sieve
of a bureaucracy, which absorbs much of the money into itself
and distributes the rest incompetently — since how could you
expect the level of knowledge and judgment among such a
cluster to be much in advance of the times? At the same time
the government attaches strings to the money, not theirs in
the first place, to those who gave it in the first place. And third,
I detest the averaging down of expectation and dedication that
occurs when thousands of poets are given money in what is
really waste and welfare, not art at all. Artists should be left

alone to paint or not to paint, write or not to write. As it is, the world is full of trash. The genuine is lost, and the whole field wallops with political and social distortions.

INTERVIEWER

Do you feel the same way about private support of the arts?

AMMONS

Not at all. Everybody who loves the arts should have the liberty to sustain the particular arts he loves, whenever, wherever. If the love and money go to the popular arts, that's the way it should be. If there is an outcry for symphonic performances of the great Bs, then that is what should be addressed. High arts that hang on almost vestigial in a culture should be addressed in their own scope, and I think they would not perish but that genius and energy would burst out whenever it's not already stifled by some blank, some holding grant, some template that just keeps blocking itself out.

INTERVIEWER

Working with you on *The Best American Poetry 1994*, I noticed that you're not exactly overjoyed at the sight of poems that have a political agenda.

AMMONS

It's not because I don't take political and large cultural matters very seriously. There are wrongs to be addressed. There are balances to be restored. The pragmatic merely supports my theoretical position. That is, what good does it do to write a poem about a matter of urgent interest that almost no one reads? In a thousand years, if it is a magnificent, not half-baked poem, enough people will have read the poem to make a difference, but by then, where are the people, what is the issue? A letter to the editor of a newspaper or magazine could be read by twenty-five thousand or twenty-five million people. It would seem patently a waste of time not to try the letter.

A more general position has to do with autonomy. One

does not want a poem to *serve* anything; the liberating god
of poetry does not endorse servitude. What we want to see a
poem do is to become itself, to reach as nearly perfect a state
of self-direction and self-responsibility as can be believably
represented. We want that for people too.

INTERVIEWER

Your short poems are lyric outbursts, and you've said that
they come forth all at once. I know that you write your long
poems in increments or passages. These seem in some ways
deliberately imperfect — casual, expansive, all-inclusive,
loose — in contrast to the shorter lyrics, which are all intensity
and compression. Do your long poems entail a different process of writing?

AMMONS

Very different. In the long poem, if there is a single governing image at the center, then anything can fit around it, meanwhile allowing for a lot of fragmentation and discontinuity
on the periphery. Short poems, for me, are coherences, single
instances on the periphery of a nonspecified center. I revise
short poems sometimes for years, whereas, since there is no
getting lost in the long poem, I engage whatever comes up
in the moment and link it with its moment.

INTERVIEWER

What's your favorite among your long poems, if you have
a favorite?

AMMONS

The poem that I like best, parts of it, is *The Snow Poems*.
It seems to me in that poem I had a more ready availability
to the names of things and to images of them than in any of
the other long poems.

INTERVIEWER

Tape for the Turn of the Year has everything to do with
the physical circumstances of its composition. You typed it

on an adding-machine tape, and this determined that you would have a poem of some length consisting of short lines and wide margins. I remember your telling me that the finished parts of the tape fell in coils in a wastepaper basket— kind of a forerunner of *Garbage*. Was this a way of reminding yourself not to take yourself too seriously?

AMMONS

Yes. That's great. That's a good connection.

INTERVIEWER

What started you going? How do you decide when to write a long poem like *Tape* or *Garbage*?

AMMONS

In 1963, when I did *Tape*, I had been thinking of having the primary motion of the poem down the page rather than across. The adding-machine tape, less than two inches wide, seemed just right for a kind of breaking and spilling. Variations of emphasis and meaning which make the long horizontal line beautifully jagged and jerky became on the tape the left and right margins. Soon after I started the tape, I noticed resemblances between it and a novel. The point, like and unlike a novel, was to get to the other end; an arbitrary end would also be an "organic" end. The tape itself became the hero, beginning somewhere, taking on aspects and complications, coming to a kind of impasse, then finding some way to conclude. The material itself seemed secondary; it fulfilled its function whether it was good or bad material just by occupying space. In many ways the arbitrary was indistinguishable from the functional.

So with the other long poems, I wrote them when I had a new form to consider, some idea that would play through. *Garbage* came from the sight in passing of a great mound of garbage off the highway in Florida. When I found a single image that could sustain multiplicity, I usually could begin to write.

Were you surprised by the success enjoyed by *Garbage*? The title is a pretty audacious gesture.

AMMONS
I'd paid little attention to *Garbage* after writing it. But there was a real spurt of interest in the first five sections after they appeared in *American Poetry Review*, so I engaged a student to type up the rest of it presentably, and I sent it off to Norton, where my editor surprisingly took it. My hope was to see the resemblances between the high and low of the secular and the sacred. The garbage heap of used-up language is thrown at the feet of poets, and it is their job to make or revamp a language that will fly again. We are brought low through sin and death, and hope that religion can make us new. I used garbage as the material submitted to such possible transformations, and I wanted to play out the interrelationships of the high and the low. Mostly, I wanted something to do at the end of a semester.

INTERVIEWER
How about *Sphere: The Form of a Motion*? You once told me that the subtitle of that poem occurred to you at a Cornell faculty meeting when somebody talked about putting something in "the form of a motion," and you liberated this phrase from its parliamentary context.

AMMONS
That's right. My application of the phrase had nothing to do with such meetings, but that was an interesting place for it to arise from. *Sphere* had the image of the whole earth, then for the first time seen on television, at its center. I guess it was about 1972. There was the orb. And it seemed to me the perfect image to put at the center of a reconciliation of One-Many forces. While I had had sort of philosophical formulations for the One-Many problem before, the earth seemed to be the actual body around which these forces could

best be represented. So when I began *Sphere*, I knew what I wanted to do. I wanted to kind of complete that process, that marriage of the One-Many problem with the material earth.

INTERVIEWER

The One-Many problem in philosophy has to do with the nature of reality, whether reality inheres in various things of which there is an infinite supply or whether there is one organizing, unifying principle that unites all the disparate phenomena. Is that a fair summation?

AMMONS

Yes. Another way that I think of it is the difference between focus and comprehensiveness. For example, if you wish to focus on a single point, or statement, to the extent you've purified the location or content of that statement, to that extent you would eliminate the comprehensiveness of things. You would have to leave out a great many things in order to focus on one thing. On the other hand, if you tried to include everything comprehensively, you would lose the focus. You see what I mean? So you have a polarity, a tension between bringing things into a sort of simplified clarity and going back to the wilderness of comprehensiveness, including everything.

INTERVIEWER

Do you feel this as a tug of war inside yourself?

AMMONS

An ambivalence, I suppose. Or ambiguity. But somewhere along the line, I don't know just when, it seems to me I was able to manage the multifariousness of things and the unity of things so much more easily than I ever had before. I saw a continuous movement between the highest aspects of unity and the multiplicity of things, and it seemed to function so beautifully that I felt I could turn to any subject matter and know how to deal with it. I would know that there would be isolated facts and perceptions, that it would be possible to arrange them into propositions, and that these propositions could be included under a higher category of things—so that at some point there might be an almost contentless unity at the top of that sort of hierarchy. I feel that you don't have to know everything to be a master of knowing, but you learn these procedures and then you can turn them toward any subject matter and they come out about the same. I don't know when I saw for myself the mechanism of how it worked for me. Perhaps it was when I stopped using the word *salient* so much and began to use the word *suasion*.

INTERVIEWER

In a few weeks I'm going to be on a panel, a symposium on the question, "What is American about American poetry?" It seems like a good question although not an easy one. How should I answer?

AMMONS

Well, I think that question addresses itself to the past and not to the present or the future.

INTERVIEWER

Do you think poetry has any future?

AMMONS

It has as much future as past—very little.

INTERVIEWER

Could you elaborate on that?

AMMONS

Poetry is everlasting. It is not going away. But it has never occupied a sizable portion of the world's business and probably never will.

INTERVIEWER

It seems that few of your contemporaries strike you as indispensable, with the exception of Ashbery.

AMMONS

Wouldn't that be true of almost any period? Of the great many who write at any time, history has kept track of few.

INTERVIEWER

Who are the few that you hold dearest?

AMMONS

Do I have to answer that? As a peripheral figure myself, I hesitate to comment on the devices of my contemporaries.

INTERVIEWER

I meant from earlier generations.

AMMONS

I would say Chaucer, Spenser, Shakespeare, Milton. I'm not that crazy about Dryden and Pope and the eighteenth century, but I like the Romantics and I like Whitman and Dickinson. That's all. That's enough. Isn't it?

INTERVIEWER

You've said many times that Ashbery is our greatest poet.

AMMONS

Ashbery has changed things for poetry in interesting ways above any other of my contemporaries. I admire almost everyone else equally.

INTERVIEWER

You are often identified as a distinctively American poet.

AMMONS

Do you find that to be true?

INTERVIEWER

Certainly your idiom is American, your conception of the poem, and I would say your relation to poetic tradition seems to me American.

AMMONS

I have tried to get rid of the Western tradition as much as possible. You notice I don't mention anything in my poetry having to do with Europe or where we come from. I never allude to persons or places or events in history. I really do want to begin with a bare space with streams and rocks and trees. I have a little, a tiny poem that says something about the only way you can do anything at all about all of Western culture is to fail to refer to it. And that's what I do. This makes my poetry seem, and maybe it actually is, too extremely noncultural. And perhaps so. I grew up as a farmer and I had at one time a great love for the land because my life and my family and the people around me depended on weather and seasons and farming and seeds and things like that. So my love for this country was and is unlimited. But that's different from a governmental assessment of things, which I believe is basically urban. And it seems to me a poet such as Ashbery who locates himself in the city, which is the dominant culture now, is more representative of the American poet than perhaps I am.

INTERVIEWER

You said you wanted to eliminate Western culture from your poetry. Why?

AMMONS

Well, I sort of disagree with it.

INTERVIEWER

With the Cartesian mind, or with what? The philosophical tradition of the West? The Roman sense of justice?

AMMONS

If I get back to the pre-Socratics, I feel that I'm in the kind of world that I would enjoy being in, but nothing since then. Especially in the last two thousand years, dominated by Christianity and the Catholic church and other religious organizations. I feel more nearly myself aligned with Oriental culture.

INTERVIEWER

I've always been curious about why you've traveled so little.
I think you spent a year in Italy.

AMMONS

Three months. We had the traveling fellowship of the
American Academy of Arts and Letters, which was for a year,
but we came back after three months. I lost twenty pounds
and I couldn't wait to get home.

INTERVIEWER

You didn't care for the experience of being an expatriate?

AMMONS

I hated it. I'm not interested in all that cultural crap. It
was just a waste of time for me.

INTERVIEWER

Maybe this is part of what you were talking about before
when you spoke of your rejection of Western culture, by which
I take it you mean more specifically a rejection of Europe or
of European cultural domination.

AMMONS

Yes.

INTERVIEWER

But it occurred to me that one reason you have traveled
very little is . . .

AMMONS

There's no place to go.

INTERVIEWER

There's no place to go?

AMMONS

Yeah, that's a good reason not to travel. Well, I'm interested in the Orient, but I'm really not interested in going there. I'm *not* interested in Europe. I have no interest whatsoever in going there. Every now and then I go to Owego and sometimes I go to Syracuse, sometimes to Geneva, Binghamton — all over the place.

INTERVIEWER

Geneva, New York, rather than Geneva, Switzerland.

AMMONS

Geneva, New York, right.

INTERVIEWER

It occurred to me that another reason might be that you'd already done a considerable journey in going from your origins on the coastal plain of North Carolina to the hills and lakes of central New York state. A critic could spin a parable about the northward progression of your life: from a state that was part of the Confederacy to a university town in . . .

AMMONS

In the Emersonian tradition. In fact there *is* an essay about how I came to the north and took over the Emersonian tradition.

INTERVIEWER

I thought you had decided to become influenced by Emerson only after Bloom told you that you'd been.

AMMONS

That's basically correct, except that I did have a course on Emerson and Thoreau at Wake Forest. The professor was basically a preacher, however, who treated the hour as an occasion for sermonizing. But yes — it's a marriage of the south to the north.

INTERVIEWER

What is?

AMMONS

The movement of my life.

INTERVIEWER

You've spent more time in the north.

AMMONS

Much more. I lived my first twenty-four years in the south.
I've been in Ithaca more than thirty years.

INTERVIEWER

Are you conscious of being a southerner here?

AMMONS

I don't hear my own voice, but of course everyone else does
and I'm sure they're all conscious of the fact that I'm southern,
but I am mostly not conscious of it. In the first years, I was
tremendously nostalgic, constantly longing for the south: for
one's life, for one's origin, for one's kindred. Now I feel more
at home here than I would in the south. But I don't feel at
home — I'll never feel at home — anywhere.

— David Lehman

Dinner at the Bank
of England

Guy Davenport

—Bank of England, guvnor? Bank of England'll be closed this
time of day.

Jermyn Street, gaslit and foggy on this rainy evening in 1901,
pleased Mr. Santayana in its resemblance to a John Atkinson
Grimshaw, correct and gratifyingly English, the redbrick
church across from his boardinghouse at No. 87 serenely *there*,
like all of St. James's, on civilization's firmest rock.

—Nevertheless, the Bank of England.

—Climb in, then, the cabman said. Slipped his keeper, he
said to his horse. Threadneedle Street, old girl, and then what?

Quadrupedante sonitu they clopped through the rain until,
with a knowing sigh, the cabman reined up at the Bank of
England. Mr. Santayana, having emerged brolly first, popping
it open, paid the driver, tipping him with American
generosity.

—I'll wait, guvnor. You'll never get in, you know.

But a bobby had already come forward, saluting.

—This way, sir.

—I'll be buggered, the cabman said.

The inner court, where light from open doors reflected from puddles, polished brass and sabres, was full of guards in scarlet coats with white belts, a livelier and more colorful *Night Watch* by a more Hellenistic Rembrandt.

The room where he had been invited to dinner by Captain Geoffrey Stewart was Dickensian, with a congenial coal fire in the grate under a walnut mantelpiece.

Captain Stewart, as fresh and youthful as he had been when they met the year before in Boston, was out of his scarlet coat, which hung by its shoulders on the back of a chair in which sat his bearskin helmet. A stately and superbly British butler took Santayana's brolly, derby and coat with the hint of an indulgent, approving smile. Whether he had been told that the guest was a professor from Harvard or whether he read his clothes, shoes and face as gentry of some species, he clearly accepted him as a gentleman proper enough to dine with his captain.

—You mean Victorian fug when you say *Dickensian*, the captain laughed. I have to do an inspection round at eleven, but as I believe I said, you're a lawful guest until then. The bylaws of the Bank of England allow the captain of the guard to have one guest, male. The fare is thought to be suitable for soldiers, and here's Horrocks with the soup, mock turtle, and boiled halibut with egg sauce will be along, mutton, gooseberry tart with cream, and anchovies on toast, to be washed down with these cold bottles, for you I'm afraid, I've been taken off wine. Not, I imagine your idea of a meal. Horrocks knows it's just right for his young gentlemen in scarlet.

—Philosophers, Santayana said, eat what's put before them.

—High table at Harvard will be amused. I'm awfully pleased you could come.

A handsome young barbarian out of Kipling, the captain's manners were derived from a nanny and from a public school and modified by an officer's mess. The British are charming among equals and superiors, fair to underlings, and pleasantly artificial to all except family and closest friends.

—But you can't, you know, saddle yourself with being a
foreigner, I gather your family is Spanish but that you are a
colonial, growing up in Boston and all that. Most colonials
are more English than the English. You see that in Canadians.
Your George Washington Irving, we were told at school, is
as pukka British as any of our authors. Longfellow also. Same
language, I mean to say.
—My native tongue is Spanish.
—Not a trace of accent. Of course you don't *look* English, I
mean American, but then you can't go by that, can you? Most
of the Danes I've seen look more English than we do, when
they don't look like Scots. You look South American. It's the
moustache and the small bones, what? I know a Spanish naval
officer with absolutely the frame of a girl. Probably cut my
throat if I were to say so, devilish touchy, your Spaniard.
Doesn't Shakespeare say so somewhere?
—I'm various kinds of hybrid. Bostonians are a breed apart
in the United States. I can lay claim to being an aristocrat,
but only through intermarriages. As a Catholic I'm an outcast,
and as a Catholic atheist I am a kind of unique pariah.
—That's jolly!
—I am, I think, the only materialist alive. But a Platonic
materialist.
—I haven't a clue what that could mean. Sounds a bit mad.
—Doubtless it is. This wine is excellent.
—No offence, my dear fellow, you understand? Our fire needs
a lump or two of coal. Horrocks!
—The unexamined life is eminently worth living, were anyone
so fortunate. It would be the life of an animal, brave and
alert, with instincts instead of opinions and decisions, loyalty
to mate and cubs, to the pack. It might, for all we know,
be a life of richest interest and happiness. Dogs dream. The
quickened spirit of the eagle circling in high cold air is beyond
our imagination. The placidity of cattle shames the Stoic, and
what critic has the acumen of a cat? We have used the majesty
of the lion as a symbol of royalty, the wide-eyed stare of owls
for wisdom, the mild beauty of the dove for the spirit of God.

—You talk like a book, what? One second, here's somebody coming. Sorry to interrupt.

Horrocks opened the door to admit a seven-foot corporal, who saluted and stamped his feet.

—Sir, Collins's taken ill, sir. Come all over queasy like, sir, and shivering something pitiful, sir.

Captain Stewart stood, found a notecase in his jacket on the back of a chair, and ordered the corporal to pop Collins into a cab and take him to the dispensary.

—Here's a quid. Bring back a supernumerary. Watkins will sub for you.

—Sir, good as done, sir.

—Thank you, corporal.

And to Santayana, picking a walnut from the bowl and cracking it expertly:

—Hate chits. Rather pay from my own pocket than fill up a form. I suppose I have an education. Latin and Greek are cheerful little games, if you have the brains for them, and most boys do. Batty generals in Thucydides, Caesar in Gaul throwing up palisades and trenching fosses. Never figured out Horace at all.

—There are more books in the British Museum about Horace than any other writer.

—My God!

—Civilization is diverse. You can omit Horace without serious diminishment. I look on the world as a place we have made more or less hospitable, and at some few moments magnificent. When would you have liked to live, had you the choice, and where?

—Lord knows. Do drink up. Horrocks will think you don't appreciate the Bank of England's port. Eighteenth century? On the Plains of Abraham. The drums, the pipers, the Union Jack in the morning light. Wolfe reciting Gray's *Elegy* before the attack, to calm his nerves. Wouldn't have thought that there was a nerve in his body. Absolute surprise to the French, as if an army had appeared from nowhere. I would have liked to have been there.

—That plangent name, both biblical and Shakespearean, the

Plains of Abraham. It was simply Farmer Abraham's cow pasture.

— Is it, now? Well, Bannockburn's a trout stream and Hastings a quiet village.

— And Lepanto the empty sea.

Horrocks permitted himself a brightened eye and sly smile. He was serving quality, after all.

— English mustard is one of the delights of your pleasant country. My friends the Russells would be appalled to know that one of my early discoveries here was cold meat pie with mustard and beer. I like to think that Chaucer and Ben Jonson wrote with them at their elbow.

— There's a half-batty Colonel Herbert-Kenny, in Madras I believe, who writes cookbooks under the name Wyvern. These address themselves to supplying a British mess with local vegetables, condiments and meat. Simplicity is his word. All the world's problems come from a lack of simplicity in anything you might think of, food, dress, manners. The bee in his bonnet is that food is character and that to eat Indian is to whore after strange gods. That's scripture, isn't it?

— He's right. Spinoza and Epicurus were spartan eaters.

— I thought Epicurus was a gourmet, or gourmand, banquets and puking?

— He has that reputation, a traditional misunderstanding. He ate simply. He did insist on exquisite taste, but the fare was basic and elementary.

— Herbert-Kenny must have read his books.

— Cheese and bread, olives and cold water. He and Thoreau would have got along.

— Not familiar with this Thoreau, a Frenchman?

— A New Englander, hermit and mystic. Americans run to originality.

— Examined his soul, did he? I heard a lot of that in America.

Horrocks poked up the fire, removed plates, replenished Santayana's glass, silently, almost invisibly.

The dormitory and the barracks had shaped his world. He was probably far more ignorant of sensual skills than an Italian ten-year-old, a virgin who would be awkward with his county wife, and would become a domestic tyrant and brute, but a good father to daughters and a just but not affectionate one to sons.

Their friendship was a sweet mystery. The British explain nothing, and do not like to have things explained. The captain had doubtless told his friends that he'd met this American who was dashedly friendly when he was in Boston, had even given him a book about Harvard College, where he was a professor wallah. Followed sports, the kind of rugger they call football in America. Keen on wrestling and track. Speaks real French and German to waiters, and once remarked, as a curiosity, that he always dreams in Spanish. Says we English are the Romans of our time, but Romans crossbred with Protestantism and an inch from being fanatics except that good Roman horse sense, which we take from the classics, and a native decency and a love of animals keep us from being Germans. Talks like a book, but no airs about him at all.

— I like this room, Santayana said. It is England. The butler, fireplace and mantel out of Cruikshank, the walnut chairs, the sporting prints, the polished brass candlesticks. You yourself, if a foreigner who reads may make the observation, are someone to be encountered in Thackeray or Kipling.

— Oh I say! That's altogether too fanciful. No butlers in America?

— Only Irish girls who drop the soup.

— Back to your being a materialist, Captain Stewart said. I'm interested.

— Your Samuel Butler was a materialist, the Englishman of Englishmen in our time. He was a sane Voltaire who was wholly disillusioned intellectually while being in bondage to his comfort and his heart, a character Dickens might have invented if he hadn't his readers to consider. The non-conformist is an English type, a paradox the English themselves fail to appreciate, for they have long forgotten that exceptions might be a threat to the community. An American Butler, even if he sounded like Emerson, would find himself too often in hot water.

— Don't know this Butler. Is *materialist* a technical term?

—The world is evident. Begin there.

The captain laughed.

—The substantiality and even the presence of the world has been called into doubt by serious minds, by Hindus, by Chinese poets, by Bishop Berkeley and German idealists.

—Extraordinary! Hindus! I daresay. And your being a materialist is your firm belief that the world is, as you put it, evident? Does all this have anything to do with anything?

Santayana laughed.

—No. What interests me is that all thought and therefore all action stands on a quicksand of tacit assumptions. What we believe is what we are and what we expect of others, and of fate.

—Here's my corporal again.

—Sir, Collins is taken care of, sir.

—Carry on, corporal.

—Sir! Yes sir!

—Spirit lives in matter, which gives rise to it. We are integral with matter. We eat, we breathe, we generate, we ache. Existence is painful.

—Do try the walnuts. They're excellent. Do you think we live in good times or bad? I mean, do you want us all to be materialists?

—I am content to let every man and woman be themselves. I am not them. When man is at last defeated and his mind bound with ungiving chains, it will be through a cooperation of science and what now passes for liberalism. That is, through his intellect and his concept of the good, just and useful life. This is, of course, a cruel paradox, but it is real and inevitable. Science is interested only in cause and effect, in naked demonstrable truth. It will eventually tell us that consciousness is chemical and the self a congeries of responses to stimuli. Liberalism is on a course of analyzing culture into a system of political allegiances that can be explained by science, and controlled by sanctions, all with the best of intentions. All of life's surprises will be prevented, all spontaneity strangled by proscriptions, all variety canceled. White light conceals all its colors, which appear only through refractions, that is, through irregularity and pervasive differences. Liberalism in its triumphant maturity will be its opposite, an opaque tyranny and a repression through benevolence that no tyrant however violent has ever achieved.

—Here here! You're talking for effect, as at the Union.

—There is no fanaticism like sweet reason. You are as yet free, being wonderfully young, and having the advantage of the liberty of the army.

—Liberty, you say?

—The most freedom anyone can enjoy is in constraint that looks the other way from time to time. You know that from childhood and from school.

—The army is school right on. And one does and doesn't long to be out. I can't see myself as a major in India, parboiled by the climate and becoming more conservative and apoplectic by the hour.

—Youth does not have as much of childhood in it as early maturity has youth. There is an abrupt demarcation between child and adolescent, a true metamorphosis.

—Something like, yes.

—The English fireside is as congenial an institution as your culture has to offer. We Americans find your bedrooms arctic and your rain a trial, but the saloon of the King's Arms in Oxford, after freezing in the Bodleian or walking in the meadows, is my idea of comfort. As is this room, as well. And as a philosopher who speaks his mind, I delight in your receiving and feeding me in your picturesque undress, those terrible uncomfortable-looking galluses, do you call them? over your plain Spartan undyed shirt. I might be the guest of a young Viking in his house clothes.

—You should hear the major on the subject of gravy on a tunic. And you decline to convert me to materialism. What, then, to believe? Horrocks and I ought to have something to benefit us from a Harvard professor's coming to dine.

—We seem to need belief, don't we? Skepticism is more than likely unintelligent. It is certainly uncomfortable and lonely. Well, let's see. Believe that everything, including spirit and mind, is composed of earth, air, fire and water.

—That is probably what I have always believed. But, look here, my dear fellow, it's coming up eleven, when I must be on parade in the dead of night, with drums and fifes. All civilians must be home in their beds. Look, Horrocks will give you to the corporal, who will give you to the bobby outside, and you're on your own. This has been awfully jolly.

—It has, indeed, said Santayana, shaking hands.

—Good night, sir, Horrocks offered.

—Good night, and thank you, Santayana said, tendering him a shilling.

The rain had let up. He would walk to Jermyn Street, keeping the image of Captain Stewart in his martial undress lively in his imagination, as Socrates must have mused on Lysis's perfect body, or on Alcibiades whose face Plutarch wrote was the handsomest in all of Greece. The world is a spectacle, and a gift.

The perfect body is itself the soul.

If he was a guest at the Bank of England, he was equally a guest at his boardinghouse on Jermyn Street, the world his host. Emerson said that the joy of an occasion was in the beholder not in the occasion. He is wrong. Geoffrey Stewart is real, his beauty real, his spirit real. I have not imagined him, or his fireside, or his butler, or his wide shoulders or the tuft of ginger hair showing where the top button was left unbuttoned on his clean Spartan undervest.

Suppose that in a Spanish town I came upon an apparently blind old beggar sitting against a wall, thrumming his feeble guitar, and uttering an occasional hoarse wail by way of singing. It is a sight which I have passed a hundred times unnoticed; but now suddenly I am arrested and seized with a voluminous unreasoning sentiment—call it pity for want of a better name. An analytical psychologist (I myself, perhaps in that capacity) might regard my absurd feeling as a compound of the sordid aspect of this beggar and of some obscure bodily sensation in myself, due to lassitude or bile, to a disturbing letter received in the morning, or to the general habit of expecting too little and remembering too much.

Four Drawings

Philip Smith

A.R. Ammons

From Strip

1.

wdn't it be silly to be serious, now:
I mean, the hardheads and the eggheads

are agreed that we are an absurd
irrelevance on this slice of curvature

and that a boulder from the blue
could confirm it: imagine, mathematics

wiped out by a wandering stone, or
Grecian urns not forever fair when

the sun expands: can you imagine
cracking the story off we've built

up so long—the simian ancestries,
the lapses and leaps, the discovery

of life in the burial of grains:
the scratch of pictorial and syllabic

script, millenia of evenings around
the fires: nothing: meaninglessness

our only meaning: our deepest concerns
such as death or love or child-pain

arousing a belly laugh or a witty
dismissal: a bunch of baloney: it's

already starting to feel funny: I
think I may laugh: few of the dead

lie recalled, and they have not
cautioned us: we are rippers and

tearers and proceeders: restraint
stalls us still—we stand hands

empty, lip hung, dumb eyes struck
open: if we can't shove at the

trough, we don't understand: but is
it not careless to become too local

when there are four hundred billion
stars in our galaxy alone: at

least, that's what I heard: also,
that there are billions of such

systems spread about, some older,
some younger than ours: if the

elements are the elements throughout,
I daresay much remains to be learned:

however much we learn, tho, we may
grow daunted by our dismissibility

in so sizable a place: do our gods
penetrate those reaches, or do all

those other places have their godly
nativities: or if the greatest god

is the stillness all the motions add
up to, then we must ineluctably be

included: perhaps a dribble of
what-is is what what-is is: it is

nice to be included, especially from
so minor a pew: please turn, in yr

hymnals, to page "Archie carrying on
again:" he will have it his way

though he has no clue what his way
is: after such participations as

that with the shrill owl in the
spruce at four in the morning with

the snow ended and the moon come
out, how am I sagely to depart from

all being (universe and all—by
that I mean material and immaterial

stuff) without calling out—just a
minute, am I not to know at last

what lies over the hill: over the
ridge there, over the laps of the

ocean, and out beyond the plasmas
of the sun's winds, and way out

where the bang still bubbles in the
longest risings: no, no: I must

get peanut butter and soda crackers
and the right shoe soles (for ice)

and leave something for my son and
leave these lines, poor things, to

you, if you will have them, can they
do you any good, my trade for my

harm in the world: come, let's
celebrate: it will all be over

Morgan Sees Euripides' *Hecuba*

Who can explain the tears in his eyes, realizing
the historical moment crossing into the present,
mountains behind the orchestra at Epidaurus,
Asclepius' cure including theatrical and medical
cleansing? Did the ducts fill in purification
or perhaps the oncoming tragedies brought pity and
fears? Mother only liked Hecuba in the first half
where the outlet was explainable grief not revenge.

Greek masses could not vary over the millennia
nor the untranslated cries be unique in time.
Morgan learned long ago that war produces monsters,
half-men, half-beastlike creatures he abhorred.
Mother could only think of the virgin's white gown.
When the mourning became murdering frenzy,
he looked out over the tens of thousands, imagining
each tragedy and finally forgiving them all.

Raped by Poseidon

Morgan slipped into the Aegean at Monemvasia
for the algae-covered rocks tried to keep him
out. He would be the first in. Mother asked:
"Why even attempt?" She saw the Venetian fortress
like Charybdis imposing herself on the bay
and the green pools of Scylla in the depths.

Morgan's body surfed over the rocks to avoid
the awkwardness of rising from the sea.

He lay on the fine pebbles pushed onto shore
then pulled out like a fickle lover.
Yet being slapped by these abusive waves
though sometimes gentle seemed a faithful gesture.

Mother would call this rock candy but stones
like hard testicles embedded themselves into
his flesh and he turned and turned over
spewing Aegean marbles into the Peloponnesian air,
but this continual rape oriented him into elements
he hardly understood; he emerged pregnant, pockets filled.

Circe's Brother

Travelers without passports may become
the norm but this Englishman remains
in Greece so Morgan asks how he lost it.
Mother at first speaks in an inquisitive way.
After a few drinks at Cap d'Or in Porto Heli
we learn of his father's wealth, his girl's abortion,
his affection for his boarding school tutors,
his sorrow at his brother's malpracticed death—
these entrance Morgan with their humanity.
Mother begins to doubt and desires to leave.
Morgan cannot move away from here.
He imagines the camaraderie between age and youth,
the country house of the dysfunctional family,
the young man's ambition for money.
Now Mother calls for the water taxi and they escape.

Rob House

Ballad of an Amateur

Now I am married there is much to despair
now that I seem to need to.
By the powers vested in me, I am
no longer about the house
playing loverboy or old Mr. Fix-it
but am placed on my horse like a ghost
and questioned about
my whereabouts there.

What I mean to say is
that by the powers vested in me,
the evening sun goes down as usual,
like a lion's head wrapped in cellophane
and pitilessly casting aspersions
on our living room and swimming pool,
on our little compact
parked at an angle in the leaves.
Not only the dry, gibbous moon but
all cuts of meat, all seeds and grains
and clutches of roughage
shake in the balance, and the earth
is small, the earth is very patient,
but the earth grows tired
of wearing our ashes on its sleeve.

What I mean to say is
now I am married there is much to despair
when the truth really is
there is nothing to dispute.
Autumn light has a way of tickling
the sides of a garage I like

or sending all the elms to the ground
now that we surround ourselves
with those things only
that are easiest to lose,
those things only elusively ours,
our floating fit and difficult joy,
now that we stand in proportion
to what we are surrounded by.
Now we begin to live our lives
as though our lives depended on them.

But the truth really is
now I am married there is much to despair
now there is cause for celebration.
Night lights elm upon elm around the house
and the cats are gone, a stunning moon
makes the swimming pool pay attention
and that is all, the moon has
the water in its power.

Robin Magowan

Looking for Binoculars

At the back of a Point Reyes ravine
Mescaline, three powdery silver piles
Poured on knife blades and then and there licked clean.
Remorse rising geometrically
Directs us ever more briskly around
Two bends and in the nick onto a bush-
Lupin meadow. Taking Ling by the arm
I guide her up to the bluff's fire-mist view.
Nausea. Urge to jettison sweaters,
Binoculars' black encumbering holes.
"Get away from me, I want to bail out."
But much as I'd like to, there is nowhere
To bail out past that imprisoning sky
The chalk-circle clouds tearing us
Leather apes in the jungle of our fears.

•

Edge to meadow ledge I roll, mouth, dagger,
Precipice, star, as each diving phaeton
Unloads its dizzy screaming sun abyss.
Electrons the size of golf balls diffract
As I wriggle to where my Circe sprawls
Elbows over eyes, black paint-spattered jeans
Rotating at washing machine frenzy.
Through the churn I hear her voice her chagrin,
"Sorry, I've poisoned you, more TNT
Than I've ever imagined." But her voice
Clatter proves too much and I roll away
Preferring my own wretched wastes and heaves.

•

To find a middle and cling: letter *M*
Well beloved of the French; Ling's navel,
Cavity into which I can intrude
All I possess of mouth, of roots. Cocooned
In exploding infancy — stars direct
To tonguelost Babel — I lie, arms twined,
Letting only my most fervent Allahhh's
Shower forth their groaning sparks. I'm reaching back
Mothering island where, what heart once knew,
Tongue sucks out: "beast," "breast," meadow's ring, Ling,
    found.

●

Each's wheel and axle we cling until
The same instant's grasslight finds us sitting
Rubbing eyes against its huge, blue-streaked blades.
Do I make out the song the brothers sang
Approaching the well? Yet everything is,
I know, because everything startles so:
The drops on the flower, the brook in the wild.
Do you pull me into sunlight, your touch
Making wax grow stronger? Behind lupin
I stand relieving myself, head in hands,
Invisible legs vibrating like stalks.

●

Time, Ling announces, to leave that blue place.
My shoes stand up, their laces tied and all.
Jeans are sparkling blue on pink gravel road.
Arms seem to limp at sides, but this may be
Because I can't focus on my fingers
Lost in the mist prism; nor the roadway
Though like a sleepwalker I recognize
A blue balustrade curving to my right.
Useless to ponder what is dream, what walk;
After that wriggling in wet ghostly grass
Being erect is miracle enough.

●

"Where are your binoculars?" Ling's question
So out of the blue has me frantically
Combing the bluff as if I've mislaid them.
I'm set to drop into the poison oak
Below (they could have rolled over the ledge)
When she adds, "Your other pair is lost too."
Back we walk, a hole with a head, two heads,
Looking for a hole between there and here.
And a title, as much an afternoon's
As a hotel sign, comes into focus.
Looking for binoculars: falling off
Of hole. Finding them: standing by a well?

•

At the meadow edge a conflagration
Of sunset-lit poppies drops us to knees.
I have Ling's hand, this future fire power,
Might binoculars prove superfluous?
On elbows, kids at a concert, we sprawl.
While Ling paints I scan her fingertip,
Pink hemisphere of the desires, as if
A stroke might reveal the gold of my face
Beckoning from lily pad to the swamp's
Cleopatra. But the comparison
Palls among the waning light's still unfound
Binoculars. Bluff's glistening of wind,
Crashing of assassin waves, as we comb
The holes of our earlier foot pressings.
Through spray, her dejected "I can't find them"
As crashings foam around. Alone again.
A roaring, a black cataract of stars.
An afternoon, two bodies pulling one
Another through, lies on its back, blown up.

•

"Hurry!" stars are all quavering as one.
But deep in a wind-proof ravine I pause
Transfixed by a pool the moonrise's Ping-
Pong is furling to an undersea grotto.
Below, miniscule brass buttons startle.
Across, soil leathers, alderbark grays merge.
Swaying together, they rise in a mushroom-
Bright fountain, separate, subside. Textures
Glisten: moon taffeta; cow parsley bells
As cathedral stalks bend in the glow and eyes
Fastened to that reel spool from blank to bank.
I'm not disconnected from anything
But my heart's peals, my sea-anemone arms
Writhing with each pulse and calling it night
Deeper ebb, purple, I can't pierce beyond.

•

Shadows like a liner's bows docking veins.
But I want to remain out so long as
The least firelight sings in my pupils.
There, branch low in the gloom, wobble winged
Flutter of a first whip-poor-will. Thrashing
Through a glitter of reeds, feet panic
Drowning. I burst onto a knoll over
The Pacific's radiator-like coils
Purple kelp sticks agleam like jagged glass.
Then the surf starts to heave away from me,
The red lights of the naval station spit
And needing a refuge I choose the roots
Of a monstrous cypress. Wrapped in parka
I lie, only my eyestraws inhaling
The radiances, pink, red, white, blue-white;
Not constellations, but glittering webs

As if each sky shepherd had alignments
It tenders to those harbored in its mist.
I let their jellies drip through my members
Until I am arrayed enough to stand,
Stalk my way back through the sabering night.

George Bradley

Opus

They cut off hands and composed cantatas;
They gutted their neighbors like fish and released
The shape of spirits from bonds of ebony;
They buried populations in pits, seeking the proper word.
They herded women into shivering lines
And raped and stabbed upon convenience.
They burned anything they found susceptible of flame,
Performing that miracle play, *Apocalypse*, every day.
Undaunted, they swallowed the hearts of enemies.
Unmoved, they confirmed dead men in the true faith.
They killed or were killed and always,
Above the smoking city, the vast lake tinged with blood,
There rose a little tune that seemed its own creation,
A lullaby, an anthem, seductive serenade.
Victims, they could be made to suffer—
It was their stock in trade,
Their competence and true possession, the good
They offered, bargaining with fate—
Victims could be broken, equated with the earth,
Starved to shadows and given to the night, and yet
Survivors could not keep from song,
Or never long, would not leave off their burden,
Brave quaver amid ruins.
Melody attended them like misery, because
The bloodlust was the song,
Its sound another kind of killing,
Because the violence and invention were as stops
Along a scale, and it was all a sort of music,
An instinctive rendering, an exuberant attack,
The one coherence snarled enough to answer

In their case: poor connoisseurs of panic,
Their cornered frenzy held the key, and naturally
They could not be restrained or ever end
That common urge and compromised relation,
The uncaring air which they called art
And by which they excused themselves.

Three Poems by Ansie Baird

What We Have Done

My mother shrugged off life
Three thousand miles from Paris,
City of her birth. It takes
Two weeks of bureaucratic tape
Before I fly her scant remains
From Buffalo to this historic place,
May 9, 1975, a fine night
For being scattered, if ever
There was one. Coconspirators,
We creep beneath the Pont Neuf,
My mother and I, she beneath
My coat in a cold container,
and then dump her in the Seine,
As I promised to do.

How her dozing old bones
Must gape at the ancient stones.
How surely my mother laughs
At what we have done, laughs
To have come home like this,
Laughs and laughs from her sandbar
In the Seine where she lies
Like fragments of an old ghost,
The ashes of a medieval saint,
In the mud of her resting place.

Getting There

Yes, like you, I too have been summoned
by an urgent phone call from someone
whose name I never knew
and I have taken the very next plane
alone to a strange dark city on a January night,
New Year's Day as it happened, and
I too have stood on the concrete island
at the massive airport terminal flagging down
unwilling limousines, all chrome and glass,
and have been driven at last down looping roads,
through unfamiliar towns and neighborhoods
to the wrong entrance of an unfamiliar hospital
where I have walked the long hallways, carrying
my lug-heavy suitcase close to midnight
down unlit passages and into incorrect elevators,
past empty nurses' stations where only the blue
blinking light of some translucent tubing
indicated there was a soul alive and I have entered
swinging doors marked Do Not Enter,
marked Isolation, marked Intensive Care,
and I have arrived alone in my black wool coat,
my suitcase dragging at my shoulder,
and have turned into one small square of light
to find one weary nurse waiting for me there
and she has gently taken my baggage
from my hands and placed it in a safe space
just behind her metal desk and I have shed
my winter coat and scarf and gloves and boots,
placing them in the sterile vestibule,
and donned the sterile paper gown and clumsy
sterile paper covers for my shoes
and I have stuffed my long blonde hair inside
the sterile cap not unlike those motel shower caps
and I have tied a gauze mask up above my nose
and down below my mouth, around my throat,
and like you I have done all this alone and

very late at night, as you have done,
and have stepped in, numb and bewildered,
to the final sterile cell where,
all but unrecognizable, bloated and bald,
my sister lies heaving in her wounded flesh.
And I leaned over her then, finally, tenderly,
and stroked her shaven head and called
to her through all those corridors of pain,
as you have called.
Clare, I have said. Open your eyes, I have said.
Look, I have said. I am here.

The Long Trek

I murder my own grandmother   stuff
her corpse in my top bureau drawer
among my underwear   nightmare of
tiny folded body like a lamb's
limp lifeless limbs   eyes closed
but not in sleep   in death among
my underpants   my mother calls to me
from somewhere else   perhaps downstairs   perhaps last year before she
disappears and enters my top bureau
drawer among all those vast spaces
in the cellar where she greets my
father hunched beneath the furnace
humming his one tune   "Some Enchanted
Evening"   off-key as usual and something stirs in the steamer trunk   it is
my only sister   back again and grimy
from the long trek out of the earth.

— Que si tu fueras el novio de mi hermana, te hubiera matado.

Mas vale todo que el callarme aquel día me costó la salud; pero no quise darle; no sé por qué habré sido. Me resultó extraño que me hablaran así; en el pueblo nadie se lastima a decirme la verdad.

— Y que si te tropiezo otro día rondándome, te meto en la plaza por la feria.

— ¡Mucha chulería es esa!

— ¡A ~~poco~~ pinchazo!

— ¡Mira Estirao...! ¡Mira Estirao...!

Aquel día se me clavó una espina e en un costado que todavía tengo clavada. Por qué no la arranqué de aquel sustento es una cosa que ~~no~~ aún hoy no sé...! Andando el tiempo, de esta temporada, que por ~~separar otras fechas~~ vino a pasar mi hermana en casa el fin de ~~unos~~ Chanfaina, mi canto ~~aquellas palabras; cuando el Estirao llegó aquella noche a casa de la Nieves a verla a la 8, como la llamó aparte:

— ¿Sabes que tienes un hermano que ni el hombre ni es nada?

— ¿Y qué se adelanta, como los enseñe en cuanto oye voces?

Mi hermana salió por defenderme; pero por poco de valió; el hombre había ganado, sé había creído a ~~ref~~ que la única vida que tendrá por no irme a mi infierno.

Camilo José Cela

The Art of Fiction CXLV

Born in 1916 in Iria Flavia, a hamlet located in La Coruña,
Galicia, Spain, into a wealthy family descended from Italian

and English immigrants, Camilo José Cela later moved with his family to Madrid, in 1925. In 1936, the year the Spanish civil war broke out, the twenty-year-old Cela completed his first work, Treading the Dubious Daylight (Pisando la dudosa luz del día), *a book of poems. After being wounded in service, Cela spent a brief period of time during his convalescence as an official censor. Then in 1942, within the panorama of despair and chaos of postwar Spanish life, he secretly printed his first novel,* The Family of Pascual Duarte, *in a garage in Burgos. The novel sold out before the authorities were able to confiscate it, and met with immediate acclaim both by readers and critics alike. The event was so spectacular that today it is accepted as the starting point of Spanish postwar literary history. Cela consolidated his reputation as a novelist and writer by producing a few other works of great merit, including* Those Passing Clouds (Esas nubes que pasan), The Galician and His Crew (El Gallego y su cuadrilla), Rest Home (Pabellón de reposo) *and* New Wanderings and Misfortunes of Lazarillo de Tormes (Nuevas andanzas y desventuras de Lazarillo de Tormes), *and his first travel book,* Journey to the Alcarria (Viaje a la Alcarria). *He also proved himself to be a multitalented artist, producing a series of paintings and drawings, and appearing in a few movies.*

Throughout these years, Cela earned his keep primarily through journalistic collaborations in various newspapers and magazines. 1951 proved to be a crucial year in his literary trajectory, the year he published — in Argentina because it had been prohibited in Spain — his literary masterpiece, The Hive (La Colmena). *The official censors, angered by their inability to derail Cela's brilliant and influential literary career, expelled him from the Press Association, which meant that his name could no longer appear in the printed media. But Cela continued unflinchingly and produced two more novels,* Mrs. Caldwell Speaks to Her Son (Mrs. Caldwell habla con su hijo), *and* The Blonde. *He then considered it advisable to remove himself from the heated atmosphere of Madrid, perhaps remembering the fate of other intransigent Spanish writers such as Federico*

García Lorca. He left the Iberian Peninsula and installed him-
self and his family — his first wife, Rosario and his son, Camilo
José — on the island of Majorca, choosing against the exile to
which many other Spanish writers of the period had resorted,
and founded the literary magazine Papers from Son Armadáns
(Papeles de Son Armadáns, *Armadáns being the neighbor-*
hood in which Cela lived). For however heated the climate,
it was not able to impede Cela's investiture into the Royal
Spanish Academy in 1957. The years he spent in Majorca were
fertile and saw the production of such works as The Rose (La
Rosa), Slide for the Hungry (Tobogán de hambrientos), Secret
Dictionary (Diccionario secreto), St. Camillus 1936 (San Camilo 1936) *and* Officiating Tenebrae 5 (Oficio de tinieblas 5).

After serving king and country in 1977, the year he spent
as a royal senator, Cela decided to take full advantage of having
won his own war against Franco's regime and its pesky censors.
Not wishing to alter the image of the mischievous enfant terr-
ible that he had had so much fun acquiring, he wrote a daring
book full of scandalous language titled Chronicle of the Extraordinary Event of Archidona's Dick (Crónica del cipote de
Archidona). *This was followed by another book along the*
same lines, an irreverent version of the classic La Celestina.
After gleefully thumbing his nose at the ancien régime, Cela
turned serious once again and in 1983 he produced Mazurka
for Two Dead People (Mazurka para dos muertos), *a structur-*
ally complicated and masterful story of love and death set in
Galicia during the time of the civil war, which earned him the
Premio Nacional de Literatura in 1984. In 1986, he returned to
the region of La Alcarria to write New Journey to the Alcarria
(Nuevo viaje a la Alcarria). *However this second trip was not*
made with a backpack and on foot, but instead in a Rolls-Royce
complete with a sculptor's model as chauffeur.

Cela went on to receive every prize of merit in Spanish
letters; in 1987 he received the Premio Príncipe de Asturias
de las Letras for his overall literary work, and in 1994, the
Premio Planeta for a new novel, Saint Andrew's Cross (La cruz
de San Andrés), *and in 1989 he was awarded the Nobel Prize.*
Yet it wasn't until 1996 that Cela finally won Spain's most

128   CAMILO JOSÉ CELA

*prestigious literary award, the Premio Cervantes, due in part
to a penchant for ruffling feathers and his indefatigable insis-
tence on being the indomitable and singular Cela.*

INTERVIEWER

You have said that often literature is "a deception, yet another fraud in the long series of frauds to which human lives
are made subject." Was your attempt to write "without subterfuge" the reason for such stark novels as *The Hive* and *The
Family of Pascual Duarte*?

CAMILO JOSÉ CELA

Well, I don't know if that was the reason, but I don't think
a writer can permit himself subterfuges, nor tricks, nor camou-
flage, nor masks.

INTERVIEWER

You have won a host of literary awards, including the Premio
Nacional de Literatura, 1985, the Premio Príncipe de Asturias,
1987 and the Premio Planeta, 1994, among others. I would
imagine the Nobel Prize of 1989 is the one that has given
you the greatest satisfaction?

CELA

Actually, I have won very few prizes. I am one of the least
awarded Spanish writers; it just so happens that the prizes I
have won are the important ones. But yes, of course, winning
the Nobel was a great honor.

INTERVIEWER

Your Nobel speech was dedicated to the literary work of
the painter José Gutíerrez-Solana. He is an illustrious painter,
and although his literary work is not very well known you
seem to find it of considerable merit.

CELA

Yes, that's right. I admire both his pictorial and literary work. I have always said that every page Solana has written has its corresponding reflection in his painting or every painting corresponds with a reflection in his literature. If you don't immediately find the reflection, just keep looking and you will find it eventually. Solana was an extraordinary writer who created six books—magnificent pages. But unfortunately Spain is such a poor country that it doesn't lend itself to having two ideas issuing from one single person. If a person is a good writer, then he can't play bridge well also. Or be a magnificent golfer. No, it just isn't done. It is obvious that, in the case of Solana, this is an absolute lie because he was a great painter as well as a great writer. But as a writer, no one paid any attention to him, which is a pity because his work is truly remarkable.

INTERVIEWER

Saul Bellow once wrote that you put yourself in a paradoxical position by attacking literature and then writing novels. What is your opinion?

CELA

Well, perhaps he is correct, I don't really know. I believe that literature is always a subterfuge. Truman Capote, who was a friend of mine, once interviewed me for a weekly that was published in Tangier called *España*. He told me that he would have liked to have written *Mrs. Caldwell Speaks to Her Son*. But it cannot matter to a writer what others say of him. Bellow may be right, but I don't really know.

INTERVIEWER

Many critics claim to have found an existentialist backdrop to your work; man is in the end responsible for his actions. However, Bellow considers there to be little theory in your work, that you are not trying to convey existential, sexual or political messages.

CELA

And he's right, without a doubt.

INTERVIEWER

Do you feel then that a writer has a social responsibility toward his readers?

CELA

No, he has a responsibility before himself and his own conscience. He must have a very great sense of his own conscience, be very aware of himself.

INTERVIEWER

Would you agree with Bellow that in your frankness and lack of squeamishness in detailing the harshest of human landscapes your work can be compared to that of Jean-Paul Sartre or Alberto Moravia?

CELA

I'm not sure. Well, yes, they both were friends of mine, above all Moravia. It's a pity that Moravia was never given the Nobel because he certainly deserved it. I think the things we writers say about each other are simply an extension of what we would like to be true, but that perhaps are not completely accurate. Also, there exists a certain responsibility — the commitment I just mentioned — to your own conscience. There is nothing more grievous than a writer who is at the service of a master. It's really a horrible affair. Because afterwards, the writer has no choice but to swallow his own work. Look what has happened to the work of the artists who were under Stalin's charge. Under Stalin's or under anyone else's for that matter. The other day someone called a piece of information to my attention which had been taken from the *Guinness Book of Records*. The human being to whom the greatest number of statues has been raised in the entire world is Stalin. He would give the order, "Make me a statue!" and they had to continue making them. Only to find that later they all came crashing

obstreperously to the ground! It's sheer nonsense and one
shouldn't allow it to happen.

INTERVIEWER

Then a writer should never allow himself to become captive
to an artificial perspective or situation?

CELA

Look, there is nothing more ridiculous than, for example —
I won't give any names — but let's just say the writer who charac-
terizes himself as "progressive," or who feigns poverty but
actually has more money than all of us. It's an affectation!
One day a woman, a very elegant French woman told me,
"Your lifestyle and tastes are akin to those of a banker." I
told her, "Well, I'm not a banker and I haven't got a red cent,
nor do I need one. I have enough money to live comfortably."
And why must I act as though I were a poor man? Be careful,
because this would be nothing more than hypocrisy. And if
I would give you the name of the writer I have in mind, you
would tell me that I'm right. But he is rather vexed with me
at the moment, so I won't mention his name.

INTERVIEWER

You have defined your goal in literature as being "to touch
the ulcer with your finger" and "write without the poultice
of rhetoric." Is this in keeping with your idea of "literature
without subterfuge"?

CELA

Well, that's my aspiration. If I achieve it or not, I don't
know. But it is certainly one of my intentions.

INTERVIEWER

What would you consider the greatest praise and the most
painful criticism you have received?

CELA

Everything has been said about me; I have been called a genius and I have been called mentally deficient. At least one of the two charges must be erroneous!

INTERVIEWER

Does it bother you to be called mentally deficient?

CELA

No, no. One cannot be dependent upon these things, or one wouldn't be able to show one's face in public. The writer— well, I speak for myself, not for others—writes according to what he thinks he wants to say. Later, if he is correct, or if he is mistaken, well, that is another problem. But you cannot take the attitudes of the reader or the critic too much to heart, or you will lose yourself. It's very clear.

INTERVIEWER

Then a writer must learn to harden himself to such commentaries?

CELA

No, it's just the way a person is. I don't think it's a matter of hardening yourself. It's an attitude. What matters to me more is the consideration I may have for myself. That worries me very much. Again, there is this phenomenon called the conscience. If I go against it, then my conscience feels remorse. But anything referring to the conscience of others is very sub-jective. Between the numerous readers that any writer may have, you will always find a variety of opinions to suit every taste. Every reader sees the same thing in a different way, often with good intentions and frequently coerced by the at-mosphere that surrounds him. But for any specific subject, however miniscule it may be, there are always diverging atti-tudes. They cannot be kept in mind when writing.

Do you feel that your work has been properly understood by the reading public?

Perhaps in Spain it is the case, but outside of Spain I really don't know. Obviously, translations are always difficult and as the saying goes, *traditore, traittore*; a translator can also be a traitor, although not deliberately, and often subconsciously. I have seen some translations that are absolute nonsense. But it is impossible to look after them. First of all, I don't have sufficient knowledge of all foreign languages to be able to do so, nor does anyone. Secondly, I don't have the time to do so. And thirdly, it simply is not worth the effort. In the prologue to the Romanian edition of *The Family of Pascual Duarte* I go so far as to say that all translations should be forbidden. I say it paradoxically, but it is also true. It's impossible to say in one language what you are saying in another. For example, a Spanish *ventana* is not the equivalent of a French *fenêtre* or an English *window*; they are all different things. There is a nuance that covers each language.

Isn't it true that your maternal language was English?

Well, I spoke English before Spanish, but I don't speak it anymore. My mother was English and my grandmother — her mother — was Italian and lived in Spain. After my grandfather died they tended to speak Spanish because it was easier for them. So, English lost ground as the family language and in the end disappeared altogether.

Have you been able to read any of your English translations?

CELA

Yes, I have read some of them, and they are not the worst of the lot. The North American Anthony Kerrigan did some very good translations. But then of course we did them together in Palma de Mallorca. We used to meet once a week. He would make a list outlining the doubts he had as they arose, and when we met we would discuss them at length. That's how a good translation is done. If not, when the translators aren't completely familiar with the language they are translating from, they go directly to the dictionary. A dictionary is too cold. There are so many nuances that can't be found in a dictionary, and translations based on them are simply not good ones. In general, the French and English translations are not bad. The bad translations are the German ones. I don't speak German, but Spanish friends of mine who speak German have told me that they're pretty bad. It's unavoidable. One day I received a book of mine translated into Chinese and I couldn't even make out which book it was. That produces a certain sense of stupor. I thought that perhaps the person who sent the book was playing a joke on me and it wasn't really one of my books. What was I to do? But then my name appeared on one of the interior pages in Occidental characters. Well, at least I now know it's one of mine, although I still haven't figured out which one it is!

INTERVIEWER

You once said that "in order to write books, all one needs to have is something to say, a stack of blank papers and a pen with which to say it; everything else is extraneous and nothing more than an attempt to add theatrics to the trade."

CELA

Without a doubt. I think inspiration is a refuge for poets. All poets are generally very lazy. They're loafers! Plato was right when he wanted to put colored ribbons around their heads and expel them from the boundaries of the state. Picasso once said, "I don't know if inspiration exists, but when it comes, it usually finds me working." One time a woman asked Baudelaire what inspiration was, and he responded by saying, "Inspiration is something that commands me to work every single day." And Dostoyevsky said, "Genius is nothing more than a long, sustained patience." What a person has to do is sit himself down before a stack of blank papers, which is in itself terrifying. There is nothing as frightening as a stack of blank pieces of paper and the thought that I have to fill them from top to bottom, placing letters one after the other. And for that reason I have the feeling that I want to say something and that what I have to say is worth being said. Of course, one must have confidence in the fact that writing, like a child in school, "I will not talk during class" one hundred times, well, simply is not literature.

INTERVIEWER

Do you still write longhand or have you modernized with a word processor?

CELA

Yes, I always write longhand. The truth is I don't know how to type and I don't have a computer. There is a computer in the house, but my wife uses it, not me, because I'm afraid it will give me cramps. It's true! Confronted with such machines — computers, even automobiles — I'm like a person from a very remote and distant area. I look at them distrustfully and don't touch them for fear that they may give off sparks. It seems very convenient for my wife, and I'm happy for her, but I prefer to write longhand. Whether I use a fountain pen, a ballpoint pen, a pencil, or a marker is all the same to me. I'm not superstitious or maniacal about such things. One young journalist asked me once, "Do you plan on writing until you don't have anything more to say?" and I responded by saying, "No, until I no longer have anything to write!"

INTERVIEWER

Would it be true to say that you are preoccupied with a search for the Spanish identity, the essence of the Spanish existence as a society lost in a certain decadence resulting from the memory of a splendorous past?

CELA

Yes, but my interest is not something deliberate. I mean to say that I don't specifically look for it, but that I inevitably tend toward looking for it. Look, I'm half Spanish, a quarter Italian and a quarter English, and my great-grandparents were Belgian. This causes me to gravitate towards a certain vision of Spain; I see it perhaps less as a Spaniard than as a Hispanist. For example, I love the Spain which the Spaniards themselves don't like: Spain of the flies, the town bullfighters, the priests, the civil guards with their tricorns, the garrotes . . .

INTERVIEWER

A vision of the *España negra*.

CELA

No, it's not truly *negra*. It's not any more *negra* than any other country.

INTERVIEWER

Or perhaps the *España árida*?

CELA

Well, arid, yes. But pardon me, all the south of Italy is arid and so is Greece and the entire Mediterranean region. Let's not get lost in stereotypes. I've never lived in the *España árida*. I live in the north of Spain, in Galicia, which is of another color. We, the Galicians, have a country that is the same color as Belgium or Holland. In exchange for this color, we cannot go out of the house without an umbrella. I have just returned from the wedding of the Infanta Elena in Seville, where the sun shone radiantly and the temperature was magnificent. In exchange for this, they don't have water. But what is there to do? That shouldn't surprise anyone, because it is already known that things have always been this way.

INTERVIEWER

Has it ever occurred to you to write about the life of the Gypsies? Or perhaps you have been tempted to write a lovely romance with heroic characters and a happy ending?

CELA

Well, no, I haven't. In a book of mine that Picasso illustrated I think there may be a romance, but I don't remember it. I believe I speak of a Gypsy as well. I have this vague idea, yes, I think so. There are Gypsies in Spain and one cannot ignore their presence. There is a very curious problem with the Gypsies. Well, it isn't really a problem, but the *payos* — we are the *payos* — are racist and completely reject the Gypsies. But be very careful, the Gypsies reject us all the more emphatically. The Gypsy is rigorously racist and doesn't consider himself a part of our way of life. He doesn't involve himself in our lives. He's more like a spectator. A friend of mine, a Gypsy, once told me that we — the *payos* — are disgraced because we have to work in order to live. They don't. By stealing a hen, they already have the problem solved for a day, and tomorrow certainly another hen will fall from somewhere. The Gypsies don't usually do military service, neither during wartime nor at any other time since they don't figure within the census. However during the war, the Spanish civil war, which I fought in, since it caught me when I was twenty years old, there was a Gypsy in my regiment who told me one night, after the day had seen a particularly heavy amount of fighting, "How appalling your war is! You *payos* have really made a mess of things this time!" They didn't kill him, but they could have. He said to me, "Look, what does any of this have to do with me?" And he wasn't wrong. What was he doing there? They had caught him and within an hour dressed him in a uniform and sent him off.

INTERVIEWER

Do you agree with Pío Baroja's statement that "art is not a series of rules, but life itself; the spirit of things as they are reflected in the spirit of man?"

CELA

Yes, of course, naturally. Don Pío Baroja was always right and in this case pointedly so. Yes, I think it's very clear. You cannot be subjected to rules. Then writing wouldn't go beyond being a mere ability. Rules can be found in soccer or any kind of sport and in the end they prove nothing more than a certain ability. Great art is differentiated by the fact that it is constantly in the state of being created. Any professor could say, "This book doesn't follow the rules of grammar." But what does that matter if you are creating new rules? Once Unamuno was told, "The word you use cannot be found in the dictionary." He responded by saying, "That doesn't matter, it will be." You see?

INTERVIEWER

And you have never, in any moment, felt something akin to insecurity or doubt regarding your abilities?

CELA

Never. Look, my mother's side of the family was rather Victorian, and we received a very rigorous upbringing. We lived with my grandparents, and there was a great difference between the way the boys and the girls were treated. The boys could do anything they wished except for a few things. We couldn't lie or tattle on a brother or a friend. But almost anything else was acceptable. We lived in the Galician country-side, and one of the things my family would never accept was when I came home crying with my head beaten in from a fight with another boy. The theory was that if a boy from this family was going to get into a fight, the injured person had better be the other one. It was inconceivable to my family to think in any other terms. Therefore, I had a certain inbred sense of security in myself. Believing in yourself creates self-assurance. For example, I was given an honorary doctorate in Sarajevo and both my wife and the then minister of foreign affairs, Francisco Fernandez Ordoñez, said, "You can't go there, it's full of snipers." But I said, "Let's see, this is a war between the Bosnians and the Serbs. I'm Galician. Therefore, they aren't after me." "Yes, but if you're there, they might hit you." "No, they won't hit me, they will always hit the other guy." I fought in a war and I must say that war is actually quite beautiful. Excuse me, war with conventional weapons. It's like a rugby game a little *a lo bestia*. It's lovely. And this war is between Bosnians and Serbs and I'm Coruñés. Why would they want to shoot at me?

INTERVIEWER

I guess you have a point, but I certainly would not want to be the one to put it to the test! But if I could ask, what would you consider the most important quality of a writer: his artistic vision, the form or the content of his work?

CELA

Well, content and continent, essence or form is an age-old discussion of which I am not in the least interested, because essence and form are one and the same thing. Literature is nothing more than words, and it is within these words that the idea resides. There is not a single word in all the languages of the world that doesn't have a meaning. Therefore, why look for the fifth leg on a cat? It's just that way. No, essence and form, content and continent are all one and the same thing. It's like the question of using a technique or not using a technique. It's not necessary even to consider it! It's similar to the need for a certain kind of scaffolding in order to raise a Gothic cathedral. Later the scaffolding disappears. Either they take it down or it falls down by itself.

INTERVIEWER

Can a writer be pardoned for certain aspects of his work that may not be quite up to par, if the overall work has merit?

CELA

No, his lack of quality is unpardonable, because then he should have dedicated himself to some other trade. For example, he could do something useful, like registering baggage in train stations or dancing with female tourists and making a living off of them. On the other hand, that would be a very noble trade. I haven't dedicated myself to dancing with tourists, well, first of all because I am no longer of an age to do such a thing, and secondly because I haven't had the proper conditioning, otherwise I would have loved it. Making a living off of flirting with women would be a magnificent trade.

INTERVIEWER

So then a writer must be willing to die of hunger, or he should change his occupation?

CELA

That's right. One should never allow oneself to be conditioned by anything. Absolutely nothing should influence you and even less the favors of power or money. There is another consideration to keep in mind: the writer can earn money in this world, but he should never propose it to himself first. If the aim is to earn a lot of money, one sets one's sights too low and never rises from a certain kind of poverty. But if one writes what one wants and later finds that there are whatever number of readers interested in hearing or reading it, the money will come as a result. But it happens without searching for it, or it may never happen.

INTERVIEWER

You are fundamentally an experimental author. What has led you to experiment so much in novelistic techniques—curiosity, artistic need or discontent with existing techniques?

CELA

Well, there is nothing more undramatic than a writer who repeats himself, or who becomes a mere caricature of himself, not to mention the writer who transforms himself into his own death mask. When I published *The Family of Pascual Duarte* and the series of notes that describe my wanderings

about Spain, *Los apuntes carpetovetónicos*, which contain a
more or less conventional vision of Spain — *la España negra*,
if you wish — it became obvious that I would always have been
able to enjoy great success in following that style. But I simply
couldn't persist in it. No, and I repeat, there is nothing more
painful, more bitter, than to become your own death mask.
A very important Italian painter became aware in his mature
years that his paintings were not selling. He understood that
people continued to look for the paintings he did as a youth.
So he began to copy the style of his younger years. How bitter
and appalling! I suppose it must be a terrifying feeling, and
therefore to avoid it one must experiment with various paths.
If one of these paths serves for someone who comes after you,
then let them continue along it. After all, the paths belong
to everyone; they're open to us all, no? All themes are fair
game. I think it was Flaubert who one day was asked by a
youth presuming to be a writer, "Maestro, if only I had a plot,
I would be able to write a novel." "I will give you a plot,"
Flaubert said. "Let's see, a man and a woman love each other,
period and end of story. Now develop it yourself. With talent,
you will be able to come up with *The Charterhouse of Parma*.
But you must put forth the talent." One day a writer, a young
writer, approached me complaining that he didn't have the
proper resources that would allow him to write. I told him,
"I will give you one thousand pieces of paper and a fountain
pen as a gift. If you have talent, you will write *Don Quixote*
on one side and *The Divine Comedy* on the other. Now go
ahead and write, and we'll see what happens, although you
probably will not turn out such works." It's very dramatic,
but also very true.

INTERVIEWER

Then you believe that talent is God-given, or I suppose one
could say, genetically rendered?

CELA

I don't really know, but evidently either one has talent or
one doesn't have it. Talent as applied to whatever you wish.

I don't believe in absolute talents, I believe in talents—oh I don't know what the adjective would be—but a talent for one thing or a talent for another. Either you have a minimum of talent, or there is nothing that can be done about it. Time cannot substitute for lack of talent. For example, how long would it have taken Velázquez to paint *Las Meninas*? Perhaps a month? If I were given six years to paint the same work, would it have come out the same? No! We could stand for six years before a canvas and would never have the same results.

INTERVIEWER

Do you believe in muses?

CELA

No, absolutely not. I spoke of this before. This is nothing more than a subterfuge used by lyric poets. It's just so convenient. It's a lie. The excuse is used not when a good piece of writing is being turned out, but when a good piece is not forthcoming.

INTERVIEWER

One of the results of your experiments in literature is that you have destroyed many novelistic myths. Has it been your intention to do so?

CELA

Not at all. When someone attempts to go against something he usually does so independent of his own will.

INTERVIEWER

Which do you consider first, the technique or the content? That is to say, first do you think about the technique that you wish to experiment with or do you already have the story and the technique comes about as the necessary form of resolution?

CELA

The technique is not deliberate. I once said, and I maintain, that in order for a woman to have a child it is enough that she is of a determinate age and that she has consented to certain amorous episodes. Later, she gives birth to a precious son or daughter with two ears, blond hair or brown, who is smart and a veritable delight. This woman may not know a word of gynecology or obstetrics, nor does she need to. She may even be illiterate! It doesn't matter! This woman doesn't know a word of genetic theory, she has simply reunited the adequate conditions of age and circumstance, and I repeat, she has a delightful child. A novel happens in exactly the same way.

INTERVIEWER

Then you sit down with your pen and write whatever comes to mind?

CELA

Yes, that's right. I sit down before a stack of blank sheets of paper—which, again, is an absolutely terrifying experience—and I begin to write. If nothing occurs to me, I remain seated at the writing table until something finally does come to mind. If I got up and started walking around each time nothing occurred to me, I would probably spend long spells pacing about. Beware of such things! You must surrender yourself to a discipline. People often say, "Writers have the immense luck of not having a boss." That's a lie. I have as many thousands of bosses as I do readers. Be careful! Because the day the readers open their hands and let go of me, I will be overtaken with cramps.

INTERVIEWER

How many hours a day do you spend before the stack of paper?

CELA

Now I spend less time, but I used to spend eight, nine, sometimes ten hours a day writing.

INTERVIEWER

Now that you have so many commitments it must be difficult to find hours for writing.

CELA

No, there is more than enough time for everything. The important thing is not to waste it. People tend to waste their time. I don't mean only the Spanish, but everybody. I write a daily column for the *ABC* newspaper in Madrid. Nobody ever sees me carrying papers and running around with airs of being all fussed. Nobody has ever seen me that way. Dr. Marañon, to whom I am very indebted, once told me that when people asked him how he was able to fulfill the many demands on his time, he would say that he was a time ragpicker. He didn't waste a single minute. Not a single one! One should never adopt these kinds of airs of being tormented, "Call me, I'll give you my phone numbers . . ." No! I have no more than one telephone and I don't even answer it. There's no need whatsoever for me to do so. When I'm at home and the telephone rings, even if I'm right next to it, I never pick it up.

INTERVIEWER

Then why have a telephone at all?

CELA

Well, so that someone else in the house can pick it up.

INTERVIEWER

Which writers do you consider to have exercised the greatest influence on you?

CELA

All Spanish writers who have written before me, because we all come from each other. Also, those who have written in languages that are unknown to me, or whose work I have not had the chance to read nor have the intention of reading in the future nor even have the slightest knowledge of their existence. There is something which is called "influence of scope." Albert Camus shared the expression with me when we published *The Stranger* and *The Family of Pascual Duarte* within a very short period of time. There were a host of doctoral theses that attempted to demonstrate that *The Family of Pascual Duarte* was influenced by *The Stranger* and the same amount of theses attempting to prove that the opposite was true. He was dying of laughter when he said to me, "When we published these novels, nobody knew who we were! Nor did we know each other. Nobody knew us!" We were two very young writers, he being slightly older than I, but by a very little bit, and we were completely unknown. But the wise men come out to give their opinion [*simulating the voice of an academic*]: "The influence is marked . . ." What are they talking about? It's so annoying. But yes, all the Spanish writers who have come before me, and if you wish, all those in all languages, even if I don't understand them, have influenced me. Literature is like a race run with torches. Each generation bears its testimony to the point it desires, or to where it is able, then passes it along to the next. Then their part is over. There is no more to it than that. Anything else is mere dramatics.

INTERVIEWER

I think it was García Sabell, the Galician writer, who said that your "soul has a profoundly ironic baggage that could possibly come from the mixture of Galician and English blood." Perhaps that is where you get your sense of humor?

CELA

Well, Galician and English humor are very parallel, if not identical. It's not a very deliberate humor, as is that of the Andalusians who truly have a sense of humor that could be considered popular. The Galician humor is more ironic than comical and is very similar to the English style of humor. For example, in Galicia there are—or there were—lawyers who were called *silveira* lawyers. The *silveira* (blackberry bush) grows along the country roads in Galicia. These lawyers acted as arbiters in disputes that would arise between fairgoers and vendors over the prices of goods. A *silveira* lawyer was paid fifty centimes, which in those days was worth one peseta, and he would give his opinion regarding the argument. The decision made by the *silveira* stood. One day in my village a *silveira* was listening to an argument between a fairgoer and a vendor and he said something that only a Galician could understand. He said to the vendor, "Yes, indeed you are being fair with your price. But only a little." A Catalan or a French person would never understand this kind of humor. It could be a typical anecdote of Bernard Shaw.

INTERVIEWER

What about the Basques, would they understand this type of humor?

CELA

Even less. The Basque sense of humor is very immediate and even infantile. The Basques belong to a race that is of the most ancient, but intellectually it is not one of the more solvent of Europe or even of Spain. As is the Andalusian, without a doubt.

INTERVIEWER

In your work there exists a certain duality in form: the content may be very harsh yet the style is always light, with a beautiful lyrical quality. Would you consider this duality another Celan irony?

CELA

Yes, perhaps, but I repeat, it's not deliberate.

INTERVIEWER

It comes from the writer's ironic baggage?

CELA

It is a result of his moral, ethical and psychological baggage.

INTERVIEWER

And, as is your case, a certain mixture of bloods?

CELA

Yes, and even if this mixture didn't exist, I simply do not believe in deliberate literature. With this, I think I could respond to all of your questions. I mean, if I would sit down before my stack of papers and write a novel deliberately, it would never work. For *The Family of Pascual Duarte* I first created an outline. I have since lost it and it's a pity. But before I even finished the first chapter, the protagonist had gone off somewhere else. When a character is created well, he doesn't obey the desires of the author, but instead escapes him. The character does what he wants. Then the writer follows behind him, writing down what the character does, never knowing ahead of time what the character is going to do next. It's like what happens in dreams, when suddenly there is a situation within the dream that produces a great change. You had no idea where the dream was going. The person who was dreaming had no idea what was going to happen. That is similar to the life of your characters. The trick is to portray them skillfully and there you have the novel.

INTERVIEWER

Francisco Gómez de Quevedo is a master of irony. I know you say that you are the fruit of all writers who have come before you, but would you agree that he has particularly influenced your work?

CELA

Perhaps of all the illustrious literary ancestors, Quevedo would be my closest relative. More than Cervantes. I feel that Quevedo is the most important writer in the Spanish language and very difficult to equal. He is extraordinary. I never tire of reading Quevedo.

INTERVIEWER

In *The Hive* you situate some of your characters in the Quevedo barrio in Madrid. Does that have anything to do with your admiration for this writer?

CELA

No. The Quevedo barrio is so called because they have built a small square and put a statue in the middle of it. There is no connection there.

INTERVIEWER

You once said that you consider yourself the most important novelist since the generation of 1898 and that it horrifies you to consider how easy it was for you to reach that position — "I must beg your pardon for not having been able to avoid it."

CELA

Oh, I said that as a joke. My aim was to irritate a journalist from *El Pais* newspaper. That's what that comment was all about. I was only thirty-something when I said that.

INTERVIEWER

But you seem to enjoy irritating people. You have quite a reputation for it.

CELA

Irritating people? Well, there is nothing funnier than a person who is irritated.

INTERVIEWER

Then you do some things deliberately after all!

CELA

Yes, yes, well, I used to do it a lot more! Now of course I don't do such things since I am what people call an older gentleman. I will turn eighty-one next year! But before, in a cabaret or some such place, when I would see a very serious gentleman sitting at a table smoking a cigar and not bothering anyone, I would look at him and begin to do this. [*He makes a gesture raising the right side of his upper lip.*] I would keep doing it throughout the night. Finally, the man would get up and go to the bathroom to look in the mirror because he thinks something is wrong with his own lip! I would continue on and finally drive the poor man absolutely mad.

INTERVIEWER

You commented once that you suffered a lot while writing *The Hive*.

CELA

Yes, and I'm still suffering. The fact is that writing is difficult work for me.

INTERVIEWER

You mean that writing is something that causes you to suffer?

CELA

I have a foundation where all my original manuscripts are kept. It's the only foundation in the world that contains the entire body of a writer's originals. If you go there someday, you will find that all my manuscripts are replete with scratches and scribbles. I suffer while writing. But I also delight in writing. When I am trying to conquer a determined situation where it hasn't occurred to me in what direction I need to move, I don't jump ahead of it or leave it for later. No. I don't continue until I have resolved the problem. So you will see in some of my manuscripts that I have written dates in the margin, marking days when I have written no more than three lines. Very few lines, but that doesn't matter. I will never have to touch them again.

INTERVIEWER

Where is your foundation located?

CELA

In Padrón, Iria Flavia in La Coruña. Padrón is the seat of the city hall, the municipal village. Iria Flavia is a hamlet about two kilometers away as you follow the road that leads to Santiago.

INTERVIEWER

Is it true that before sending a manuscript to an editor you read the entire work aloud in order to polish it?

CELA

Not exactly. The case is that when I write I do it aloud. Many faults and cacophonies that the ear is able to catch cannot be seen on the written page. So, if it sounds poorly to my ear I can catch the error. Sometimes it takes me quite a long time to discover what isn't working, that a word is lacking or that one needs to be taken out, but I insist on searching for it and finally finding what's wrong; that there is a word missing or that a comma isn't placed correctly, etc. It comes from listening. And one must, naturally, write as best as one is able. I will allow someone to say that in one of my pages there is something that is not well done. What is there to do? But it's the best that I have been able to do because I always put the greatest interest in my five senses. If it doesn't come out better, well, all the worse for me.

INTERVIEWER

Would you allow an editor to make changes in one of your manuscripts?

CELA

No! He would be flying out the window in seconds flat! Never — be careful in this — never! The Spanish editors are respectful of such things, the European editors are in general. But the Americans are not so respectful. Well, there are many different kinds of editor. But I think the American authors allow it. In Spain, France or England it would be inconceivable. An editor would never dare to say something to an author because they know the author would pick up and move on to the neighboring editor.

INTERVIEWER

One of your literary trademarks is *tremendismo*, which has been defined as a mixture of "dirty realism" together with certain techniques taken from Joyce, Proust and Dos Passos and something vaguely related to existentialism.

CELA

Let me ask you this, does any of that matter? Not a bit! And the critics say and the professors say . . . let them say what they want! Look, all of us must make a living at something. They take one of my books and say, "This is how it is." Let them say whatever makes them happy! What does any of it matter? Bah!

INTERVIEWER

All right, then I will ask you if you see humans as being truly as perverse and the world as cruel as you portray them in your books? I mean, are there no redeeming factors to life?

CELA

Well, I'm sorry but I see it as I portray it in my books. Because I don't pretend, I make no pretenses, and it's truly horrifying.

INTERVIEWER

Do you believe that society is what perverts man or is man already perverse *ad ovum*?

CELA

Well, I wouldn't take it too far, but in general, I believe that society is what is perverting. I believe in the individual and not in syndicates, that's very clear. I don't believe in congregations, nor religion, nor political parties. I believe in the individual.

INTERVIEWER

Then that goes along with what you said before, that a writer must be wary of the favors of money and power, maintaining himself always on the outside of any conglomerate or institution.

CELA

Yes, that's right, always. I am very much in agreement with that.

INTERVIEWER

Although you write about the degradation of the human condition, one can see that you have a certain affection for your characters and sympathize with their plight. I will go so far as to say that one can even sense a certain optimism. You would at least admit to that much, wouldn't you?

CELA

Well, I'm not sure. I don't feel that the human beings whose fate it has been to live in times such as these have too many reasons for optimism. Humanity has pretty much come unhinged. But I, individually and humanly, am optimistic. I believe that we will end up crawling out of the ruts. I remember when I was wounded in the war . . . I still have fuselage in my body which my wife and some crazy doctor wanted me to have removed. I refuse! It has been in my body for over fifty years, and the only thing I must be careful not to do is walk in front of a store that sells magnets or I'll end up stuck to the windows! But when I was wounded and in the hospital I was able to hear, although I could neither see nor speak, a doctor say to the nun, "And this poor boy, for the short amount of time he has left, give him the best you have." And I thought, "But I'm as good as a rose!" I thought it, but I couldn't say it. I was more than half-dead, more like three-quarters dead. Well, that happened more than fifty-some years ago, and here I am! And still in pretty good running order at that!

INTERVIEWER

And still putting up a pretty good fight . . .

CELA

Yes, and as I have already mentioned I will turn eighty-one next year. I'm very proud of that. And do you know how many years older than my wife I am?

INTERVIEWER

No, not exactly. I know that your wife is very young.

CELA

Well, how many do you think?

INTERVIEWER

I'm not sure, perhaps about thirty years older?

CELA

No, forty-one. Well, forty at the moment because she has just had a birthday, but on May 11 I will once again be forty-one years older than her.

INTERVIEWER

You are very well preserved. Who has more energy, you or your wife?

CELA

She does. She fucks me so that she can tire herself out a bit.

INTERVIEWER

Do you find it rejuvenating to have a wife that is so much younger than yourself?

CELA

Well, I don't know. I am certainly pleased with how things are now. She has me working very much . . .

INTERVIEWER
Would you say that you have the heart of a *pícaro*?

CELA
No, no, I wouldn't say that. I would say, however, that I have a vision of Spain similar to that of an English tourist.

INTERVIEWER
It almost seems as though throughout your entire work the true protagonist is Spain itself.

CELA
Perhaps you're right. Maybe that is true. Spain is a very wide, manifold and varied country. You must see that yourself.

INTERVIEWER
Which of your works would you consider the most important?

CELA
Ah, well, I don't know. It's all the same to me. I haven't read a single one, so I can't really say. No, I haven't read a one of them and I haven't the slightest interest in doing so. I think it's enough that I write them. There is nothing in the world more stupid than the writer who turns himself into his own Buddha and goes through life looking down at his own belly button.

INTERVIEWER
When *The Hive* was published in New York you were immediately expelled from the Colegio de Periodistas and your name was prohibited from appearing in any official newspapers. From that time forward you had to fight the iron fist of the official censors.

CELA
Yes, well, they didn't censor *The Hive*; it was entirely prohibited in Spain.

INTERVIEWER

Knowing that you were threatened with censorship, did you ever change your writing or self-censor?

CELA

No, that never occurred to me. I knew full well that I would eventually stumble over the censors but it was just the same to me, and anyway I knew that in the long run I would win the battle, which is precisely what happened. Also, throughout the years the Franco regime was in power, it never became a regime of strength, but stayed a regime based on force. Which is not the same thing. A regime that is supported only by the police cannot resist; it will not stand. There is no theoretical structure holding it up, and there wasn't in Franco's case. The Nazis had a theoretical structure, the Fascists, the Communists, Stalin, Hitler and Mussolini all had one. But not Franco. Franco just went along, maintaining, which he was successful in doing for forty years.

INTERVIEWER

You never went into exile as many Spanish artists found it necessary, or at least preferable, to do. But you did distance yourself from the mainland by spending many years on the island of Majorca. Was that a conscious decision to escape too direct a confrontation with Franco's regime?

CELA

No, not really. I went to Majorca for other reasons. I just didn't want to be in Madrid. I spent many years in Majorca, perhaps thirty or more.

INTERVIEWER

They were very fruitful years for you.

CELA

Yes, well, if you continue to work, after a time you realize that quite a heap of pages has accumulated.

INTERVIEWER

You had a very active public presence during the difficult
years after Franco died — during the period of the transition —
and were named by King Juan Carlos I as a senator in Las Cortes
Constituyentes in 1977, where you participated in drawing up
the Spanish constitution. It must give you an enormous sense
of pride to have contributed in so important a role to the
history of Spanish democracy.

CELA

Well, my role was minimal, but certainly it is a beautiful
experience to help in generating a constitution. What's more,
it's a constitution that is functioning in Spain. That's really
something because in Spain constitutions have this tendency
to last but a very short time. This one is working. One time,
after being in a senate session for eight or nine hours — and
I was more bored than an oyster, but I felt it was my duty to
be there given the fact that the king had named me to the
position and I had accepted as, well, as an obligation — I started
to nod off a bit. The president saw me and said, "Senator
Cela, you are sleeping." Of course, I then woke up, or halfway
woke up, and said, "No, Mr. President, I was asleep." "It's
one and the same thing, to be asleep or to be sleeping," he
said. So I responded by saying, "No, Mr. President, it's not
the same thing at all to be screwed as to be screwing." And
it's true, it's not the same thing at all, is it?

INTERVIEWER

I'm sure the president must have loved having his grammar
corrected so astutely!

CELA

Well, it's the answer that occurred to me at that moment!
Perhaps on a different day nothing would have occurred to
me at all. It's just that he gave it to me so easily that the
response would probably have come out by itself.

INTERVIEWER

It seems as though the books you wrote based on your *vaga-bundeos* throughout Spain, which you call your *apuntes car-petovetónicos*, sprout from the same disquiet of the generation of 1898, and Unamuno's search for the *España eterna*.

CELA

Yes, and a desire to flee the cities. That also interested them. Myself, I live in the country.

INTERVIEWER

You prefer country life over the city?

CELA

Absolutely. I live in the country and I have always lived in the country during my entire life whenever I have had a choice in the matter. Walter Starky, an Irish gentleman and director of the British Council in Madrid, also walked all over Spain carrying a violin.

INTERVIEWER

A violin?

CELA

Yes, yes, he played the violin and spent a lot of time with the Gypsies.

INTERVIEWER

Journey to the Alcarria stands out in this series. Your charac-ters seem to react to the sophistication and overacademicism of city life. Would you qualify them as sort of actively anti-intellectual?

CELA

No, not really. The *vagabundeo* is actually quite literary in Spain and in other areas as well.

INTERVIEWER

And you have returned to the Alcarria, but this time as a very elegant vagabond.

CELA

Yes, in a Rolls-Royce. But I no longer have the Rolls, now I have a Bentley. I have come to realize that a Rolls is only for Arab sheiks or Texas oilmen. The British royal family and I drive Bentleys.

INTERVIEWER

And the attractive young mulatto chauffeur, is she still with you?

CELA

No, she is not with me any longer. Now my wife drives. The authorities took my license away.

INTERVIEWER

Really? For what reason?

CELA

Well, I simply do not agree with the traffic regulations. But since they are laws . . . the idea of having to put on a safety belt and stop at intersections and such nonsense. They say you must stop and look when at an intersection. No. I once said to a judge, "I know very well that the law cannot be subjected to reason, but I will demonstrate to you on a blackboard that the Chinese theory is true: the shorter amount of time one spends at an intersection—you must accelerate!— the less chance there is of having a collision." They told me that I was wrong and, well, since they denied the evidence, I burned my license and that's that. This happened after I ran into a Biscuter, a small two-seater that used to be manufactured in Spain. There were five people in the car. All five were killed, naturally.

INTERVIEWER

All five of them?

CELA

Well, I feel very badly about it. I had a Jaguar then. I am limited to lamenting the affair, but they were five very stupid people. They were completely drunk, in a small car that was turning off a small road onto the main highway. No, no. It was horrible. And after killing them, well, of course one feels sorry about it. Well, at least a bit sorry. Perhaps less than what you might think! Hey, be careful with how you write this up, they're going to think I'm a savage.

INTERVIEWER

Don't worry, Mr. Cela, I'll be careful with what I put in the interview.

CELA

No, just say that there were only four people in the car . . . oh my, this is really horrible, isn't it? How appalling.

INTERVIEWER

In your latest novel, *La Cruz de San Andrés*, which won the Planeta award, the protagonist and narrator Matilde Verdú takes us through the "chronicle of a collapse," the headlong fall of certain characters into abjection and the most absolute poverty, insanity and social degradation. She writes her chronicle on La Marquesita, a brand of toilet paper.

CELA

Well, she used various brands of toilet paper; La Marquesita was the best of the bunch . . .

INTERVIEWER

Yes, but why did she write on toilet paper?

CELA

Oh, for no reason. Any psychiatrist would be able to write five hundred pages looking for a good reason.

INTERVIEWER

Then you did that out of a kind of solidarity for unemployed psychiatrists?

CELA

Oh yes, one must help other people out, no?

INTERVIEWER

You often incorporate into your work a highly sexual and scatological content that many people consider excessive. What do you think about that?

CELA

Well, I think that's just fine. Look, I'm not going to criticize the critics. Let them say whatever they wish because it's all the same to me.

INTERVIEWER

How do you feel about the current panorama of Spanish literature?

CELA

Well, I'm neither a critic nor a literature professor.

INTERVIEWER

But it seems as though Spanish writers are coming into vogue, especially in France and Germany.

CELA

Perhaps they are becoming a fashion, but it is all fomented by the ministries of culture. I'm not interested in any of it. It's all bureaucracy.

INTERVIEWER

Is there any writer who stands out in your point of view?

CELA

Quevedo. Yes, Quevedo.

INTERVIEWER

Well, Quevedo's work perserveres and remains very contemporary.

CELA

You bet. Quevedo is much more contemporary than all these young octopuses.

INTERVIEWER

But is there any young writer who has captured your interest?

CELA

Quevedo, Quevedo.

INTERVIEWER

Have any of the younger writers come to you seeking advice?

CELA

No, no. They wouldn't dare. I would throw them out the window.

INTERVIEWER

But if they would dare, would you give them advice?

CELA

No, I would not. I don't give advice to anyone, let each person make his own mistakes.

INTERVIEWER

You once dedicated an edition of one of your books to your enemies. Do you have many enemies?

CELA

Oh yes, and they have so helped me in my career. You must learn how to foment your enemies. It is good for a writer to foster his enemies.

INTERVIEWER

You mean that not only should a writer have enemies but that he should actually cultivate them?

CELA

Yes, so that they help him move up the ladder. I would love to be able to say what a certain powerful Spanish general of the nineteenth century once said. He was regent, a captain general and president of the government. When he was on his deathbed, the priest who served as his confessor said, "General, do you forgive your enemies?" And the general responded, "No, no, I don't have any enemies." "But General," the priest exclaimed, "what do you mean you don't have any enemies after holding the positions of power that you have held?" The general responded, "No, I don't have any enemies because I've brought them all before the firing squad." I would love to be able to say the same thing, but no, I haven't had the strength to do so. I'm just a poor, simple man, no?

INTERVIEWER

Are you working on any project for the near future?

CELA

No, not at the moment. But you must understand that books are not something that you project. A novel does not exist until it is published and in the hands of the readers. Until then, it is pure phantasmagoria.

INTERVIEWER

You must have a million ideas swarming around in your head.

CELA

Ideas? My head is full of them, one after the other, but they serve no purpose there. They must be put down on paper, one after the other.

—**Valerie Miles**

From The Tangier Diaries
1962–1979

John Hopkins

1964

January 5

Tangier is a lax place. Too much dope and too many servants. Food is fresh, booze is cheap, and rents are low. In other words, paradise!

January 6

I believe in man alone, astride the horizon. Go on, take the next step—get lost in the desert!

January 7

Today so blue. A sea and sky to defy Matisse. A few white buildings and a lone tree seem to speak of impending solitude as I prepare to leave for the Sahara.

January 8

People go into the desert for a number of reasons. To be terrified, to be purified, to experience what the French call the "baptism of solitude." I go to be alone and lonely: to force myself to experience that. Also to see muscles contract under skin and over bones. And to throw off the burden of living comfortably among friends and doing the same thing every day.

January 12

First night out — Casablanca, Hôtel George V, Avenue de la Grande Armée. 10 dirhams [about $2.00]. Clean.

The feeling of melancholy induced by traveling by train at night revives childhood memories of lying in a hospital ward, also at night. You are alone among strangers, confined to a space you cannot leave. Your fate is in the hands of others. There is a helplessness or passivity in both situations.

January 14

Tiznit, Hôtel Belle Vue. 8 DH. Wonderful!

Yesterday a fifteen-hour bus trip from Casablanca — fifteen hours of continuous theater. At least 200 Moroccans with their children and animals must have gotten on and off. And the land becoming drier and the horizon more distant and heat distorted as we head south.

January 14 1/2

Sleepless in Tiznit.

Here is unbroken flatness beyond the ramparts. The wind is blowing: the dust is swirling and entering everywhere. The Anti-Atlas Mountains shimmer in the distance.

Before you can say you have lived, you have to sit around African bus terminals at five o'clock in the morning.

January 15

Tafraoute, Hôtel Salama. 6 DH. Filthy.

Living on oranges, black bread and tea.

Paul [Bowles] has given me a letter to a tribal princess who owns a fortress in these mountains, but I can't find her. Only one bus per week goes anywhere near her Kasbah, and it left yesterday.

In crowded Paris I found being alone an agony. In Africa, where nature dominates, I am all right. Yesterday, wandering in the mountains around Tafraoute, I spied a flock of goats in a valley below. The wind bore the sound of a flute. Out there among the red rocks . . . complete silence. Now I know why the Greeks idealized him. (I never really understood until I heard his music.) He was about ten years old, in a djellaba.

Ramadan begins tomorrow.

January 16

Nazlie Nour, half-French, half-Egyptian hippy living in Tafraoute. Her wish: to stay stoned all the time. "When I'm high I feel five million years ahead — or behind — it doesn't matter — as long as it's not now." Living with her seven-year-old son, Juba. Terrified underneath, she avoids the world. Running scared from the Bomb, society, just about everything.

Leaving her house, I stepped into the ink bottle. No moon or star, not a single light shining in the village. I groped my way back to dirty sheets as invisible pariahs snapped at my heels.

January 19

Goulimine, Hôtel des Voyageurs. 5 DH. No water.

Flat here, empty, nothing. *Waloo.* I sit in my fleabag hotel room reading about Rimbaud's grandfather, waiting for to-morrow's market! Why? The smell of human shit on the wind. Ramadan — can't get any tea. Turning into an orange, I've eaten so many.

Goulimine — the garbage dump of the Sahara.

Spent last night in Tiznit at the *hammam* — one of man's great inventions. Scrubbed, stretched, flipped about like a fish by an enormous Negro. Never been so clean in my life. Saw myself in the mirror: the ribs have come back.

This afternoon I climbed a gray mountain covered with sharp reddish rocks. Place full of vipers — short fat snakes with flat heads. So lazy they didn't hiss or try to get out of the way. If you step on one it turns its head and sinks its fangs into your ankle. Be careful or you're a dead man.

January 20

Tarjijt, Hôtel ? (no name). 2 DH for a straw mat.

This oasis comes close to paradise. In the middle of a land-scape of shiny black rock — palm trees full of dates, grass, little canals, paths, sunken dikes. Little black birds with orange beaks flit through air that is both warm and cool. Few people are about and few dwellings are to be seen — palms and mud walls hide all. Occasionally I glimpse a woman in black, shoul-dering a jug of water, gliding through the palms. I hear chil-dren laughing among the trees. Water runs in little canals — *seguiat*. Having found the serpent, I'm looking for Eve. The serpent is an American mining engineer called Mr. Anderson who is about to let loose a monster — one that will strangle and crush this place. He says there is pure magnesium here. The whole area is a huge crater where a gigantic comet hit the earth millions of years ago. By some freak of nature the magnesium has refined itself — eight million tons of it and worth $32,000 a ton! Next year an American mining company, Johns Manville, is moving in. This is the way the world will end — exploited and industrialized.

January 21

Camping on jungle riverbanks in Peru left me with a fear of snakes. Last night I slept with a candle burning, lest one slither in and take me by surprise. The oasis swarms with adders, cobras, scorpions, but . . . the best dates in the world.

January 23

I keep Ramadan as a matter of courtesy, and to avoid dirty looks should I light up a cigarette to kill my hunger. *"Tu ne fais pas Ramadan, Monsieur?"* They are so strict in their habits that even a Christian must be a good Moslem while traveling in the south of Morocco during the month of Ramadan.

January 22 1/2

2:07AM (still can't sleep).

To do what Rimbaud did with his poetry, to go beyond doubt, reflections and questioning — to a level of pure sensation, to make poetry ecstasy, union with God, to become a God oneself. He failed, but he tried. He flew too high. He went to Harar; I'm in this place.

January 23

The Berbers never use *vous* when they speak French, only the familiar *tu*. From their life outdoors they have got something great which I hope they never lose, despite Anderson and his factories. He too appreciates their qualities. Hardest and most grateful workers he has ever seen. They hate Arabs (northerners). His men hid a live cobra under the clothes of a union man from Casa while he was swimming. He got the message and cleared out.

January 23 1/2

Back in Tiznit, weak from lack of food.

Saw a face this afternoon identical to the one looking out from Velazquez's *Bacchus*. The direct simplicity of these people.

January 24 Aqqa

Arrived here feeling sick, thin, wiry, strong. The Sahara: cold, windy, dusty, lonely, lovely. The call to prayer echoes from a distant mosque. Dust everywhere. The dust is six inches deep. Your feet kick up explosions when you walk. On the bus we cover our faces with black *fibrans* (turbans) to keep from choking.

Berber men squat while pissing, bearing out Montaigne.

January 25 Aqqa

This place is a ghost town. There's nobody here. I found a bed in the old Foreign Legion fort, and spread my djellaba on bare springs. Last night I shared a *tajine* with the bus drivers. The Berbers are simple, honest and fatalistic; they make us westerners seem neurotic, grasping at straws. They know that fate lies not down the road ahead, but behind us, written by the hand of God (*Mektoub*). They seem wiser and happier. They take life as it comes and — *in'shallah* — make the best of it. If I am to learn something on this trip it will be from them.

January 26
Everyone black here: high cheekbones, broad cheeks, narrow nose bridges, nostrils flaring out like funnels. These are the Haratine people, descendants of slaves dragged in chains across the burning wastes of the Sahara to work the oases of the Moroccan south.

January 28
Why does Paul live in Tangier? Because it is poised between the ancient civilization of the Mediterranean and this timeless nothingness of the Sahara. This kind of balance appeals to him.

January 31
Taroudaunt Hôtel. 6 DH. Comfortable.
This is Souss country — rich — with markets and shops bursting with produce. It is also full of *colons* — tough, self-confident French running their farms, leading a man's life, reminding me of white settlers in Kenya. I'm staying in a French hotel and, faced with lunch, I ate it — the first European meal in three weeks.
Already I miss the Sahara. What is it about that blasted lunar landscape where I felt so sick and lonely that makes me want to run back into it? How I long for a sea of yellow sand!
As I head north toward Tangier, I already feel a deep nostalgia over having left something pure behind. That purity was me.

February 6
Back in Tangier.
Returned to the Kasbah to find a letter from Sonia Orwell at *Art and Literature* magazine in Lausanne. She has accepted

my short story, "All I Wanted Was Company," for publication
and enclosed a check for $400! All thanks to Paul; he read
the story and suggested I send it in.

I went to tell Bowles the news and found [William] Burroughs. He didn't say much, just sat in the corner dipping
his hand into the *majoun* jar, like a kid eating jam with his
fingers. Later I ran into him again dining alone in the cellar
at Paname's. This time he regaled me with tales of his Peruvian
adventures. His dry laconic delivery had me shrieking with
laughter.

Many nights he sits at the Parade Bar having dinner before
the regulars arrive. He likes good food. A lonely ascetic figure
in a dark business suit, he generally eats by himself staring
poker-faced at the wall. But when I bring my drink to his
table, he always asks me to sit down. The undertaker look
puts people off, but like all writers he works alone all day and
enjoys socializing in the evening.

February 7

Dinner with the Bowleses in Jane's apartment. The sponta-
neous affection and sense of fun they share make them seem
more like brother and sister than man and wife. Their intimacy
is more fraternal than sexual. They live in separate apartments,
one above the other, and communicate by a squeaking mauve
toy telephone. Jane: "Fluffy, (squeak) come on up. John is
here. Dinner (squeak) is ready." Jane likes to cook. Tonight
it was jugged hare in a red wine sauce. It was like being in
New York except for Sherifa [*Jane Bowles's Moroccan compan-
ion*] who rattled on in Arabic in her gruff mannish voice and
laughed uproariously at her own jokes. A rough alien presence
who acted as though she owned the place. Jane — a fragile
figure like a priceless vase that has been knocked to the floor.
The pieces have been glued back together, but crudely and
the cracks show. Sherifa stood there, arms crossed, hammer
in hand.

February 8

Finished *Naked Lunch*, the wildest, funniest book I've ever
read.

February 9

Every Friday a black flag flies from the mosque outside my window. It inspires a kind of dread in me, like a pirate ship's Jolly Roger. It also reminds me how quickly the weeks are passing.

February 15

Ketama (kif capital of the world).

La Estrella del Norte (our bus) got stuck in the snow and the motor conked out. Joe [McPhillips] and I had to spend the night in a road mender's cabin. My feet were soaked until we got the fire going. Slept like a couple of dogs in front of the fire while the blizzard howled outside.

March 11

Today the Kasbah was invaded by a boatload of blazered, capped, stripe-tied, knee-socked English schoolchildren on vacation. Never saw such crazy kids. Redheaded, towheaded, thick glasses, peering gaping agog at everything from mules to Arabs. In America they would be branded as weenies, but I see no reason to worry over England's future generations. They have preserved their character, their eccentricities, their curiosity.

Outside my window sitting atop a high wall, an Arab girl, her robe in tatters, her face ravaged by syphilis, watches these healthy, affluent children and in turn is watched by me.

March 14

Paul has rented the Bonnet cliff house for the season. Jane brings food baskets from town. Tennessee Williams was there, so overcome with sadness over the death of his friend Frank Merlo that he hardly spoke.

Last night Paul, Brion Gysin, Joe McPhillips and I watched Larbi Layachi [*author of* A Life Full of Holes *written under the pen name Driss Ben Hamed Charhadi and translated from the Arabic by Paul Bowles*] make *majoun*. Larbi's recipe calls for chopped almonds and walnuts, honey from his father's beehives and a small mountain of kif. We each get a Skippy peanut butter jar full. Later, stoned, we walked to the cliff. White waves sucked at the rocks below. A big moon hanging over the Strait left a slippery track on the water.

Brion: "We're here to go."

Paul: "We're here to learn."

March 18

With Bill Burroughs in his apartment atop the Loteria Building, 16 rue Delacroix. Decrepit tables and shelves loaded with cut-ups, clippings and files. The old upright Remington looks like a dinosaur from another age. The tape recorder has only one tape: a recording of static. This comfortless place looks more like a writer's factory than an author's study.

We go onto the balcony. "This is the bridge of my battle-ship," he drawls. "From here I can see everything. See the *comisaría* down the street? Fire one! Boom! It's gone! Haw haw haw."

Mark Doty

Visitation

When I heard he had entered the harbor,
and circled the wharf for days,
I expected the worst: shallow water,

confusion, some accident to bring
the young humpback to grief.
Don't they depend on a compass

lodged in the salt-flooded folds
of the brain, some delicate
musical mechanism to navigate

their true course? How many ways,
in our century's late iron hours,
might we have led him to disaster?

That, in those days, was how
I'd come to see the world:
dark upon dark, any sense

of spirit an embattled flame
sparked against wind-driven rain
till pain snuffed it out. I thought,

This is what experience gives us,
and I moved carefully through my life
while I waited for . . . Enough,

it wasn't that way at all. The whale
—exuberant, proud, maybe, playful,
like the early music of Beethoven—

cruised the footings for smelts
clustered near the pylons
in mercury flocks. He

(do I have the gender right?)
would negotiate the rusty hulls
of the Portuguese fishing boats

—Holy Infant, Little Marie—
with what could only be read
as pleasure, coming close

then diving, trailing on the surface
big spreading circles
until he'd breach, thrilling us

with the release of pressured breath,
and the bulk of his sleek young head
—a wet black leather sofa

barnacled with ghostly lice—
and his elegant and unlikely mouth,
and the marvelous afterthought of the flukes,

and the way his broad flippers
resembled a pair of clownish gloves
or puppet hands, looming greenish white

beneath the bay's cloudy sheen.
When he had consumed his pleasure
of the shimmering swarm, his pleasure, perhaps,

in his own admired performance,
he swam out the harbor-mouth,
into the Atlantic. And though grief

has seemed to me itself a dim,
salt suspension in which I've moved,
blind thing, day by day,

through the wreckage, barely aware
of what I stumbled toward, even I
couldn't help but look

at the way this immense figure
graces the dark medium,
and shines so: heaviness

which is no burden to itself.
What did you think, that joy
was some slight thing?

Three Poems by David Lehman

Effects of Analogy

> *Poetry is almost incredibly one of the effects of analogy.*
> — Wallace Stevens

Poetry is to jazz
as literature is to music
as Lake Como is to the Arno River
or as de Chirico is to Kandinsky.

Bop is to analytic cubism
as John Coltrane is to Malcolm X
or as Patrick Ewing is to the Knicks
as freedom is to necessity.

Roy Eldridge is to the trumpet
as Dizzy Gillespie is to Roy Eldridge
or as Virgil is to Homer
or as birds are to ornithology.

Every image is to any of its particulars
as the city of Marseilles is to the whole of France
as Virgil is to Dante
or as Rodin's statue of Balzac is to the author of *Lost Illusions*.

A mirror is to death
as the first verse in Genesis is to the Gospel of St. John
or as *The Rite of Spring* is to the color green
or as a violent revolution is to a theory of mass psychology.

April in Paris with you is to Autumn in New York
as Earth is to Venus
as Eros is to Aphrodite
as the city at night is to the city by day.

The Double Agent

1.

It was going to snow and then it didn't snow.
He loved her like a dying man's last cigarette.

2.

It was cold where she was going and she was
susceptible to chills. She felt in her pocket
for her pills. She was out of breath
by the time she reached the top of the stairs.
The man waiting for her had been waiting for an hour.
"I'm sorry," she said. The man laughed.
He had all the time in the world.

3.

The kid swore under his breath.
He was young, quick, and his head was on fire.
He was going to do something great,
he didn't know what, only that it would be important.
He was born for it. His parents would love him,
and then they would give him back his childhood.

4.

The dog was planning his next betrayal.
It was, he reasoned, in the nature of dogs
to betray their bitches. The men at the bar
were wearing dark suits and ties as thin
as the excuses given by an unfaithful mate
to her homicidal husband on the phone.

5.

She ordered a manhattan for her and a martini for him.
He smiled. He hadn't expected to be working
with someone so—so charming, he said,
kissing her hand.

6.

The dog was dead. That was the message.

7.

She had the look of a woman who likes
being looked at. "How could you
do it?" she gasped. The kid paused
at the door. "It was easy."

8.

The man reading the paper in the hotel lobby
heard every word. There was a short silence.
Suddenly he put paper down.
"I am the stranger of whom you speak," he said
in the formal English of a Spaniard
in a Hemingway novel. That was the tip-off.

9.

"Enlighten me, Mr. Lane, if that is indeed your name.
Why didn't you leave at once when you could?"
"Loyalty," he replied with sarcasm so thick
you could be sure he was carrying a false passport.
In that second, he had to make up his mind:
was he bluffing, or would he pull the trigger?

10.

"Three men have been killed for those papers."
He sounded indignant. She looked bored.
She had heard it too many times before.
But she had never become used to the sameness
of hotel rooms in Alpine villages visited
in childhood dreams. She dreamed she was invisible
and could watch everyone live their normal lives,
herself unseen.

11.

When they murdered his mistress,
they made sure he was watching.

12.

He could see it from the balcony:
freedom; there it was, across the river,
in the brown haze of dusk:
a row of dead birches like the bars of a gate
with blue water and green hills behind it.
Tonight he would go. What was the signal?

13.

Was it worth it? You didn't ask yourself.
You just grabbed your case and went.
You didn't even know the date, the month
and year, until you got there. Afterwards,
if you were lucky, there would be time
to remember. Well, he would have to do
the remembering for both of them. And once
a year, in a hotel room in a nondescript town,
he would take out her photograph,
look at it, and put it carefully away.

Sestina

for Jim Cummins

In Iowa, Jim dreamed that Della Street was Anne Sexton's
twin. Dave drew a comic strip called the "Adventures of
    Whitman,"
about a bearded beer-guzzler in *Superman* uniform. Donna
    dressed like Wallace Stevens
in a seersucker summer suit. To town came Ted Berrigan,
saying, "My idea of a bad poet is Marvin Bell."
But no one has won as many prizes as Philip Levine.

At the restaurant, people were talking about Philip Levine's
latest: the Pulitzer. A toast was proposed by Anne Sexton.
No one saw the stranger, who said his name was Marvin Bell,
pour something into Donna's drink. "In the Walt Whitman
Shopping Center, there you feel free," said Ted Berrigan,
pulling on a Chesterfield. Everyone laughed, except T. S.
    Eliot.

I asked for directions. "You turn right on Gertrude Stein,
then bear left. Three streetlights down you hang a Phil Levine
and you're there," Jim said. When I arrived I saw Ted Berrigan
with cigarette ash in his beard. Graffiti about Anne Sexton
decorated the men's room walls. Beth had bought a quart of
    Walt Whitman.
"Come on," she said. "Back in the apartment I have vermouth
    and a jar of Marvin Bell."

You laugh, yet there is nothing inherently funny about Marvin
    Bell.
You cry, yet there is nothing inherently scary about Robert
    Lowell.
You drink a bottle of Samuel Smith's Nut Brown Ale, as thirsty
    as Walt Whitman.

You bring in your car for an oil change, thinking, this place
    has the aura of Philip Levine.
Then you go home and write: "He kissed her Anne Sexton,
and she returned the favor, caressing his Ted Berrigan."

Donna was candid. "When the spirit of Ted Berrigan
comes over me, I can't resist," she told Marvin Bell,
while he stood dejected at the Xerox machine. Anne Sexton
came by to circulate the rumor that Robert Duncan
had flung his drink on a student who had called him Philip
    Levine.
The cop read him the riot act. "I don't care," he said, "if
    you're Walt Whitman."

Donna told Beth about her affair with Walt Whitman.
"He was indefatigable, but he wasn't Ted Berrigan."
The Dow Jones industrials finished higher, led by Phillip
    Levine,
up a point and a half on strong earnings. Marvin Bell
ended the day unchanged. Analyst Richard Howard
recommended buying May Swenson and selling Anne Sexton.

In the old days, you liked either Walt Whitman or Anne
    Sexton,
not both. Ted Berrigan changed that just by going to a ball
    game with Marianne Moore.
And one day Philip Levine looked in the mirror and saw Marvin
    Bell.

Two Poems by Joel Friederich

The Sea Bream

The fine meat of its back
was opened, the steel flourished
with such quickness and artistry
no calligrapher could have reproduced
those translucent petals of white
chrysanthemums blossoming everywhere
from its midsection.
It was still alive,
a small and startled thing
laid on incense cedar
in the center of our feast,
and the sticky glass of its eyes
watched over a sea of food
as pieces of its living self
disappeared down our throats.
The death was a magnificent
presentation, though I'm not sure
death is just the word
because even as the eaten flesh
stirred into human form,
life leaped continually
into the hollows of the fish,
looking for a foothold.
It keeps coming back that way,
doesn't it, entering the body
even after tired years
with such quickness and artistry—
your lover's eyes across the table,
devouring; your father's last look
at the station; the first blade
of sea slicing through trees.

White blossoms open everywhere
in my midsection.
I am a small and startled thing.

Heat Lightning

My mother built a screened-in porch
with a clear view of the west
just so she could sit in a glider
and keep an eye on the slow progress
of late afternoon thunderstorms,
how they rise from the next county
and by evening swell in flashing towers.
Maybe it's become her image of death—
the long buildup when nothing happens
except blackbirds flapping over cornstalks,
the light thickening and air growing still
as even insects decide it's time
for holiness, then the sudden tearing loose
from the world and being engulfed
in a whirlwind beyond imagining.
Or maybe it's just better than anything
in the static of her TV, and a comfort
to know the worst can be survived.
Afterwards, in a cloudless night,
the western sky blinks heat lightning.
With no apparent source, it must be
electric residue swirling in the storm's wake,
images left crackling in the air
where the dying have recently passed,
the world refusing to calm down
even after you're gone.

Two Poems by Claes Andersson

In this country . . .

In this country we manufacture cages
We construct them just as you wish
made-to-order, a cage for each occasion
Ordinary cages for one but mainly
cages for two, or more
if children are involved and of course they are
Delicate little cages for use at ladies' fêtes
Everyday cages holiday cages mother's-day cages
Cages so small you can carry them with you
Extraordinarily cool cages for summer
and cozy cages outfitted for winter with everything built in
Cages so discreet you scarcely notice them
or cages you can leave in a safe-deposit box
Watertight shock-proof cages shielded against radiation
Cages with adjustable space between bars, cages on wheels
with automatic transmission and headrests, invalid cages
Cages for the sight- and hearing-impaired, supersonic cages
Cages with built-in balconies and air conditioning
Cages for the insane, for students, for seniors
Cages for infants, cages for twins
Cages for soldiers, living and dead
Cages for love, for hate, for boxing, for wrestling
Cages for home and school, religious cages
Cages are our specialty
Name the cage we cannot put at your disposal
and we will make it for you while you wait

It begins with a meeting . . .

It begins with a meeting
It's the meeting that's important—not the two
who meet
Your hands are open
I open my hands for you

      The smallest social unit is two people

Inside our cells
a peculiar half-light abides
That's where the poem comes to light
I call what happens o s m o s i s

      It happens in all directions and at once

When the wall cracks, light rushes in
Life rushes out
We are born in all directions and at once

      —translated from the Finland-Swedish by Rika Lesser

Two Poems by James Laughlin

Jack Jigger

They call me Jack Jigger because
I'm entirely made of little pieces
Taken from other people (some are
Alive, some dead). If there were
An autopsy the coroner would have
A hard time identifying which bits
I was born with, which were really
Mine. I can hear him saying to his
Assistant: "There's lot of foreign
Stuff in here, things I never ran
Across before." When I walk fast
I hear a kind of rubbing inside,
Like bits of paper rustling. That's
How it is, pieces of paper moving
Against each other. The doctor has
Tried every kind of coagulant.
But no use. He's given up on me.

The Fatal Dance

Let them twirl a dance
Of shadows, she so graceful
In the hand over hand, he
So handsome and strong.
They are much admired,
By others at the ball.

But there has been so much
Pretty dancing in days gone by.

Who remembers the dancers?
Where do they sleep now?
Who weeps them? And who
Weeps for the Buddhist monks
Who knelt quietly at Borobudur,
Arms crossed heads bent, when
The invading Muslims lopped
Off their heads? The dance of
The swords, that was a merry
Day. Dance on, dance on.
There is no end of dancing

Liam Weitz

Cats

1

I hoist the cat up in the basket of
a forty–foot–long picking pole and give

it a wild ride whipping the pole around
and around the sky. The cat can't understand

I am only somewhat cruel and so it jumps
free of the sack and claws the forty feet

of air down to the ground. It hits with a thump
and crouches momentarily stunned then leaps

and takes off at a run flat out around
and around the house racing for lost wind

as I try to stop the circling but on
the third lap it doesn't come around again.

2

Our female drags her leg to the front stoop.
She is not bleeding. We think she was hit

by a car. Mother and I move her into
a padded box and take her to the vet

who diagnoses a clean break and says
that he can pin it, put her in a cast

but the bone still may not heal. Or he could put
her quietly to sleep and save us money

and when I ask what I should do, Mother
tells me how short we are of money but

I should decide. When the doctor puts the needle
into her she growls even as her proud head falls.

3

Sometimes I take the skeleton out of its box
and when I set it by the two white cats

it seems to gather weight. The cats lick it
as though they sense the fur I feel stroking

the bones, wanting to have it back alive
so that I too can breathe. In fact I breathe

a life of sorts into the bones: they shift
and waver in my filling eyes. The ghost

of old injuries bends my body like
an ache before rain, twisting ribs to stick

out on one side, symmetry gained and lost
through violation of such simple trust.

Two Poems by David Yezzi

Beatitudes of Poverty

No single excess, nothing jerrybuilt
or squandered in a fit of thriftlessness
accounts for what we've ended with. Despite

our frugal care, the stores are sapped; red ink
replaces black. The sideboard's single fig
bites off a taunt; tea steeps from last week's bag.

Now rash displays of force are the domain
of every man persuasive in his loss,
whether forfeiture of property or just

the planned disintegration of a trust.
Ah, my dear, this blessed turnabout
has laid us open to a bitter faith.

Blessed are the keepers of contempt,
and blessed all the fallow acreage
left still unworked. We cherish our reward.

Our giving in embodies the reverse
by which we gain this holy poverty
and, with each vicissitude, a certain grace.

The Graven Image

Hundreds of people stood . . . in a courtyard of a Post Avenue apartment building to see . . . whether a bathroom window shimmered with the image of Jesus Christ or was just smudged.

— The New York Observer

Not that anyone made it, necessarily,
inlaid with enamel, cast in gold;
not painted like an ornament

or candlelit behind an altar screen.
It surfaced in the most mundane of spots,
at an ordinary hour, squibs of light

fracturing the unlikely vessel,
a window — not stained or even leaded —
just a pane of unimportant glass.

Simply appeared (Who knows how many weeks
it went unnoticed? Was it always so?):
the all-familiar image of the Christ —

long-haired, bearded like on the Turin shroud —
reflecting on the crowd that heard and came,
doubtless, to divine the glory there.

And they had known him. Perhaps it matched
the drawings in some illustrated text,
the pictures children seldom get beyond

in their barely hirsute search for holiness.
(*I* was one of those.) Or was it nearer
to the revelation witnessed on the road,

when nothing like himself, in foreign clothes,
he showed himself to several of his flock?
"Some people need a sign," the pastor said—

the inward search replaced by outward show—
as, overhead, high clouds betrayed the forms
of a whiskered face, an anvil, mountain, cow.

Katherine Beasley

The Plea Bargain

They gave me a choice I didn't want: the fate
of a twenty-three-year-old man named
   Frank Spencer Robertson,
who one March tried his best to murder me,
now sitting in the Harris County jail with his defense lawyer
and the District Attorney and a fighting hysterical mother
trying to save her own son from jail, and the D.A.
   on the phone
asking me can I live with twelve years? ten years? or eight?
And me staring at a computer screen filled with my words,
trying to decide just how low I'd go: "Ten."
And the D.A. saying: "Yes, that's good, we won't go lower
   than ten,"
then betting the defense lawyer five hundred dollars
the jury would slap him with the max: twenty,
and that Frank would be an ass if he didn't take the plea
and then telling me they needed until Tuesday to decide
so the defense lawyer could knock some sense into his mother,
force her to see they were cornered, trapped, just like me
when he flung himself at me between the parked cars
with no room to run, nothing to do but try to fight
myself loose, all the while screaming, screaming for help
from anybody who could hear, until he pushed me down
   and ran,
his tennis shoes making no sound on the pavement.
So I hung up the phone, stared into the green letters, flipped
   the switch
and watched the screen go dark, reflecting my face back
   at me now,
a face which almost slid away from this world, as they slid me
into the waiting ambulance, its red lights flashing
all over the dark trees.

((Chap2A)

Chap2a is designed to follow chap1z on Beau,pont. The idea is to
give a more straightforward narrative--BVeaumont to Yle, and then
to Millbrook and then to the private schools.

(Chapter Two

My sisters and I returned to the United States

in the late spring of 1939. My father was

choreographing his children in and out of the

lowering clouds, sending an older batch there for

the summer, and needing finally, when war broke

out, to go to St. Lis in France to pick up a

daughter and three nieces.

Before returning to the United States,
He plucked us out of boarding school after the

winter term. He saw war ahead and wished to open

our eyes to the big Italian scene. To this end he

hired a chauffeur (Valerian Bibikoff became a

lifelong friend), an Italian guide (Count Rhigini), He

and brought from the United States our music teacher

(Marjorie Gifford), whom we worshipped after five

years' exposure, three days of lessons and play

every week. We spent one month in Italy, an entire

week in Florence at the Uffizi Gallery, and the

visit to Rome included a private audience with the

freshly-inducted Pope Pius XII, who remains in the

memory as the most imposing presence ever

encountered, asceticism and resignation written

into his face. I must have been carrying thirty

A manuscript page from a forthcoming book by William F. Buckley.

© Jill Krementz

William F. Buckley, Jr.
The Art of Fiction CXLVI

William Frank Buckley, Jr., founder, editor, and now editor-at-large of the National Review *author, lecturer and host of public television's* Firing Line, *the longest-running serious TV talk show, was born in New York City on November 24, 1925. His early schooling was in England and France. He graduated from the Millbrook School in N.Y., studied at the University of Mexico, and took a B.A. with honors at Yale in 1950, where he debated, was Class Day Orator and chairman of the* Yale Daily News.

Drafted into the army as an infantry private in 1944, he was discharged as a 2nd Lieutenant in 1946. From 1947–1951, Buckley taught Spanish at Yale and in 1952 became associate editor of the American Mercury. *Then he resigned to do free-*

lance writing. In 1955, he started his own magazine and is generally held to be responsible for assembling a coherent, responsible, modern Conservative movement in the United States. In 1962, he began a syndicated weekly column, which continues; in 1965 he ran for mayor of New York; in 1966 he began hosting his weekly television show.

He was Lecturer at the New School, was a member of a Presidential Advisory Commission on the USIA, and in 1973 was appointed by President Nixon as a public delegate to the United Nations.

He has received twenty-nine honorary degrees and sixteen awards in journalism, literature and television (an Emmy). His latest, the Presidential Medal of Freedom, was awarded in 1991.

From his first, God & Man at Yale, *in 1951, to his most recent, the novel* Brothers No More *(1995), he has written 36 books and contributed to nine others, including volumes on intellectuals, Catholicism, the Beatles. It was at fifty that he first turned to fiction, producing* Saving the Queen *(1976) and in 1980 won the American Book Award for Best Mystery (*Stained Glass*). After ten novels featuring his hero, CIA agent Blackford Oakes, he produced his eleventh novel,* Brothers No More, *taking a new tack, in 1995.*

Any attempt to catch William F. Buckley, Jr. in one place at one time must fail to catch the essence of a man in motion. This "interview" is the result of a series of exchanges over a period of time. The settings were as varied as Buckley's interests and attachments.

The family's main house, in Stamford, Connecticut, is a large, comfortable old establishment with a stucco exterior, painted a surprising pink, surrounded by flower and herb gardens, tended carefully by Mrs. Buckley, and it is a house filled with flowered cushions. Books and framed photographs are everywhere. Part of the talks took place in the music room, which houses a harpsichord, bookshelves, a projection screen television set, and audio equipment. A Bösendorfer piano is visible within the house, used over the years for concerts by Buckley's friends like Rosalyn Tureck, the virtuoso harpsi-

chordist; Dick Wellstood, the jazz pianist; and Buckley him-self. Outside the big glass windows, beyond a sloping lawn, is Long Island Sound, one of Buckley's favorite sailing grounds.

Buckley's office is in the capacious garage, and overflows with papers, computer equipment, books. Over the garage is a small apartment where the Buckleys' son, Christopher, a novelist, humorist, and editor, has done some of his own writing.

The principal setting for our talks was in the Buckley's pied-à-terre, off Park Avenue in Manhattan, an elegant place, with most of the conversations conducted in the Red Room. This serves as Pat Buckley's city office — she is a formidable fund-raiser for good causes, most of them in the arts — and as li-brary, small sitting room, bar, etc. Outside in the foyer is a harpsichord at which arriving visitors are likely to find the master of the house practicing or playing for his own enjoy-ment.

It is a true Buckley place, handsome but not staid, warmly hospitable. Evidence of their enthusiasms are everywhere: again, photographs, books, as well as paintings, many by the Spanish artist Raymond de Botton, picked out by small spot-lights; a candlelit dining room; and a long salon for entertain-ing, with the aid of the Buckleys' largely Hispanic staff. Much of the daily small talk in the house is in Spanish, with English almost a second language.

Other exchanges took place by telephone, from his car, letters, faxes, and E-mail, some from the Buckley's winter place near Gstaad, Switzerland, where they spend February and part of March each year; and once from the Concorde on the way to Sri Lanka, on which plane he was leading a round-the-world tour group and which had recently suffered "the humiliating loss of one-third of its tail after takeoff from Sydney."

Despite his peripatetic existence, Buckley, an unfailingly gracious man, with a wry smile and a quick laugh, gives full attention to questions, as if he had all the time in the world.

INTERVIEWER

What sort of things had you been writing before the novels?
You tend to group your previous books into categories, yes?

WILLIAM F. BUCKLEY

The most obvious category, I suppose, is the collections of
columns, articles and essays, four or five of those before my
first novel. There were two or three offbeat books: a book on
the United Nations and the term I served there, a book on
running for mayor of New York, a book on crossing the Atlantic, which has the ocean as mise-en-scène, and then a sort of
autobiographical book on a week in my life, *Cruising Speed*.
So when you suggested that I write a novel, I had at that point
published twelve or fifteen nonfiction books.

INTERVIEWER

I remember saying you might like to try a novel one day.
The name *Forsythe* came up, and I thought your reference
was to the "Forsyte Saga" which was then on television . . .
as well as in the literature. You said, no, like *Frederick* Forsyth.

BUCKLEY

Well, my memory of it was that I had just read Forsyth's
The Day of the Jackal and admired it hugely. That the reader
should know exactly how it ended and nevertheless still pant
his way with excitement through 300 pages—I thought that
was really a splendid accomplishment. I remember saying
something along the lines of, "If I were to write a book of
fiction, I'd like to have a whack at something of that nature."

INTERVIEWER

So you liked the challenge of writing about an occurrence
in contemporary history where the reader knew the outcome
and . . .

BUCKLEY

Yes, although I proceeded not to do so. That is, *Saving the
Queen* did not have a predictable and well-known outcome,

though some of the succeeding novels did. However, I have this problem — perhaps some people would think my problem is greater than this — which is that I have never succeeded in prestructuring a book. I've never started a novel knowing what the end is going to be. When I get about halfway through — and I go into this only because I assume it's of some technical interest to other writers — I then need to stop and force myself to figure out how the Gordian knot is going to be severed, because at this point there are a lot of characters and dramatic questions that need to be consummated. Some people feel that a book comes out better written that way — if the author himself doesn't know what's going to be in Chapter Two when he writes Chapter One, Chapter Two might then be more freshly minted and read that way. I'm skeptical. It seems to me that a thoroughly competent operator would sit down and think of what's going to be in Chapter One through Chapter Forty, and simply move ahead. What I do at the end of an afternoon's work is write two or three lines on what I think is the direction of the narrative, and where we might logically go the next day.

INTERVIEWER

If you stop yourself halfway through — almost as Ellery Queen used to stop three quarters of the way through and say, "Now that you have all the clues necessary for a solution, what is the solution?" — is there a tendency then to load too much resolution into the end of a book?

BUCKLEY

I think that's a danger. It's what I hope I've avoided, in part because I'm very easily bored, and therefore if I can keep myself awake from chapter to chapter, I assume I can keep other people awake. That is why I don't reserve all the dynamite for the end. This may be the moment to say that in all of my novels — to the extent that I have a rule — my rule is to devote a very long chapter, close to the beginning, to the development of a single character. In book one it's Blackford

Oakes, which is natural. In book two, *Stained Glass*, it was
Erika, a Soviet agent. I lifted her as though Vladimir Nabokov
had a daughter, not his son, Dimitri. I confided my invention
to Nabokov, which perhaps precipitated his death. He didn't
live to read the book, but he was very enthusiastic, as you
remember, about the first book, and his widow liked *Stained
Glass*. In any event, I've always felt that the extensive development of one character gives the book a kind of beef that it
doesn't otherwise have. That's the only regimen to which I
willingly subscribe and towards which I naturally drift.

INTERVIEWER

One of the questions about your novels is: how much is
true, and how much is invented?

BUCKLEY

Well, I poach on history to the extent that I can. For instance, when I was in the CIA it was reported to me that the
evidence was overwhelming that the destruction of Constantin
Oumansky's airplane—he was the Soviet ambassador to Mexico—was an act of terrorism, executed by Stalin. Stalin was
killing people capriciously anyway in those days, so it was
inherently believable. On the other hand, as I remember,
Oumansky lived for a few hours after the plane came down,
so the explosion wasn't very efficient. Thus there's a school of
thought that sees it as a genuine accident. But for a novel I
don't trouble myself about matters of that kind. That is to
say, if something was in fact a coincidence, but might have
been an act of treachery, I don't hesitate to decide which is
more convenient for the purpose of the narrative. The books
are, after all, introduced as works of fiction. Everybody knows
that Charles de Gaulle is going to survive the OAS, and everybody knows that Kennedy is not going to survive the twenty-
second of November, 1963, and everybody knows that the
Berlin Wall is going to rise. Even so, I attempt to create suspense around such episodes. And manifestly succeed. The
books get heavy criticism, positive and negative, but no one

says, "Why read a book in which you know what's going to happen?"

INTERVIEWER
Still, it's a nice challenge of art to put yourself up against history.

BUCKLEY
Sure. And I owe that idea to Forsyth.

INTERVIEWER
In the patterns you've developed, one of them is the unspoken premise: this is the way it *might* have been behind that great event that we all know about.

BUCKLEY
That's right. I found myself attracted to this idea of exploring historical data and visiting my own imagination on them. The very successful book on the death of Kennedy written by Don DeLillo, *Libra*, does, of course, that. In a sense overcomplicated and ineffectively ambitious in some of its sections, it's a magnificent piece of work, in my judgment. As long as the reader isn't persuaded that you are trying, via fiction, an act of historical revisionism, I don't think you meet any hard resistance.

INTERVIEWER
So the reader will go with you in a combination of invention and known history, but won't accept so cheerfully an editorial.

BUCKLEY
Yes. Of course, I think it probably depends also on how contentious the theme is. For about twenty-five years, dozens of books were published to the effect that Roosevelt was responsible for Pearl Harbor. Never mind whether he *was*, in a sense, or was not, I think that if during that period a novel pressing his guilt had been written, there would have been

a certain amount of polemical resentment. If one were to write today a novel about a senator from Massachusetts and a young woman in Chappaquiddick, and how he drowned her or deserted her or whatever, readers would tend, under those circumstances, to think of it as more an effort to make the case against Teddy Kennedy, rather than as a work of fiction.

INTERVIEWER

There seems to be a period that has to elapse before you can safely . . .

BUCKLEY

I think so. At this point I think you can speculate about the death of JFK and not get into trouble. Like Sacco and Vanzetti.

INTERVIEWER

You consciously stayed away from that event for a long time.

BUCKLEY

Until novel number eight. *Mongoose, R.I.P.* flatly says that although Oswald took the initiative in suggesting that he intended to try to assassinate the president, Castro, without acting specifically as an accomplice, urged him to proceed.

INTERVIEWER

To go back for a moment to the one character you choose to develop at length: do you decide, as you're writing your way into the novel, which character you will give a full history, or do you decide that before you write?

BUCKLEY

I sometimes don't know who the character is going to be until I've launched the book, but I'm consciously looking for a target of opportunity. For instance, in *Stained Glass*, I decided that the Soviet woman spy — who is acting as a translator and interpreter for Count Wintergrin, the protagonist—was the logical person to have a complex background. So I made up the daughter of Nabokov and went through her whole childhood and love life and her apostasy from the West.

The Cold War is an essential handicap?

I hate to use the word in this context, but I must—these are novels that *celebrate* the Cold War. I don't think that's a paradox that affronts, any more than, say, a novelist who celebrates a world war. But my novels celebrate the Cold War, and therefore the passions awakened by this titanic struggle are really a narrative obligation. The fact of the matter is that in our time—in my adult lifetime—somewhere between fifty and sixty million people were killed *other* than as a result of war or pestilence, and in most cases—the great exception being the victims of Hitler—were the victims of the Communists. Now that struggle is sometimes made to look like a microcosmic difference, say some slight difference of opinion between Alger Hiss and Whittaker Chambers. In fact, it was a typhoon that roared across the land—across bureaucracies, academia, laboratories, chancelleries. One week after Gorbachev was here in New York, I found myself using the past tense about the Cold War, which shows you how easily co-opted I am. But the Cold War is the great political drama of the twentieth century, and there is extraordinarily little literature about it written in the novel form. There are great exposés— *The God That Failed*, *The Gulag Archipelago*. But if you think about the American scene, there isn't really an abundant literature, is there?

Why do you think this is so?

I think that there's a sort of feeling that much of the conflict has been an *alien* experience. Of course, there are those New

York intellectuals who are exceptions. I remember one middle-aged man who came to *National Review* a couple of weeks ago and said that when he was growing up he thought the two political parties in the United States were the Communist Party and the Trotskyist! That was all his mother and father ever talked about. Irving Kristol will tell you that the fights at the City College of New York were always on this or that modality of communism. But on the whole it has not been a national experience. When you think of Updike or Bellow or Walker Percy, and the tangentiality of their involvement in the Cold War, there isn't really a hot concern for it. It must be because our novelists disdain such arguments as grubby, or because they think that it's an ideological quarrel with no genuine intellectual interest for the mature person. But of course it has been the great struggle of our time. For that reason I think of my novels as entertainment but also as designed to illustrate important problems in that setting. It means a lot to me to say this: when I set out to explore the scene, I was determined to avoid one thing, and that was the kind of ambiguity for which Graham Greene and to a certain extent Le Carré became famous. There you will find that the agent of the West is, in the first place, almost necessarily unappealing physically. He drinks too much, he screws too much and he's always being cuckolded. Then, at some dramatic moment there is the conversation or the moment of reflection in which the reader is asked to contemplate the difficulty in asserting that there *is* a qualitative difference between Them and Us. This I wanted to avoid. So I was searching, really, for a little bit of the purity of Herman Melville's Billy Budd in Blackford Oakes. Billy Budd has no sense of humor, and without a sense of humor you can't be genuinely American. Therefore, Blackford Oakes couldn't be Billy Budd. Furthermore, I made him almost spectacularly good-looking in defiant reaction to these semidisfigured characters that Greene and Le Carré and Len Deighton specialize in. I got a little tired of that after novel three or four, so I don't belabor the point as much.

Your reference to Graham Greene. Does he matter to you?

BUCKLEY
Graham Greene always struck me as being at war with himself. He had impulses that he sometimes examined with a compulsive sense to dissect them, as though only an autopsy would do to dissect their nature. He was a Christian more or less *malgré soi*. He was a Christian because he couldn't quite prevent it. And therefore he spent most of his time belittling Christianity and Christians. He *hated* the United States, and his hatred was in part, I suppose, a reaction similar to that of some finely calibrated people to American vulgarity. But with him it was so compulsive it drove him almost to like people who were professional enemies of the United States. And since the most conspicuous critic of the United States in this part of the world during the last twenty-five years has been Fidel Castro, he ended up being, God help us, pro-Castro. He once gave the answer — it might have been in *The Paris Review*, I forget — to the question, "What is the word you least like in English?" *America*. And he set out to prove it. Given the refinement of his mind, it's always been a mystery to me that he should have been so besotted in his opposition to that towards which he naturally inclined — Christianity and all that Christianity bespeaks — in order to identify himself with those he saw as the little men. Okay, but when the little men were such people as Fidel Castro or Daniel Ortega? It all defies analysis.

INTERVIEWER
Who else among the people practicing this kind of fiction do you pay attention to?

BUCKLEY
Well, I'm not a systematic reader. I read a little bit of everything. I've never studied the achievement of any particular author seeking to inform myself comprehensively of his tech-

nique or of his point. I occasionally run into stuff that deeply impresses me. For instance, Updike's *The Coup*, which I reviewed for *New York* magazine. It astonishes me that it is so little recognized. It's *the* brilliant put-down of Marxist Third World nativism. It truly is. And hilarious. It's a successor to *Black Mischief*, but done in that distinctively Gothic style of Updike's — very different from the opéra bouffe with which Evelyn Waugh went at that subject fifty years ago. And then I think that Walker Percy's *Love in the Ruins* is another *1984*. An exquisite extrapolation of what life might be like if we didn't dominate technology, and yielded to totalitarian imperatives. He combined in it humor with a deep and often conscious explanation of human psychology via this vinous character — the doctor — who dominates the novel so convincingly.

INTERVIEWER

Somehow, for some unannounced reason, we are talking about Christian novelists. I'm struck by this only because the much remarked phenomenon of the 1950s, 1960s and 1970s has been — certainly in America — the Jewish novel, or the novelist who writes from a background in Jewry.

BUCKLEY

That reminds me that along about 1951 or 1952 — whenever it was that Graham Greene wrote *The End of the Affair* — one critic said, if Mr. Greene continues . . . if he writes one more book like this, he must thereafter be evaluated as a *Catholic* novelist. He didn't say Christian novelist. And indeed Greene's succeeding book was a rather sharp departure. It occurs to me that the point you really make is more nearly about Christians who write novels, not Christian novelists. G.K. Chesterton, Hilaire Belloc and Wright Morris *were* Christian novelists. But Updike is a Christian who writes novels. A reading of his work wouldn't permit you to decoct from it, with any sense of certainty, that the author was a professing Christian. I don't think from *Love in the Ruins* you could guess Walker Percy was a Catholic.

INTERVIEWER
I was thinking about your own deep religious faith.

BUCKLEY
Well, yes. I'm a professing Christian, and every now and
then I take pains to let the reader in on the fact that so is
Blackford Oakes. On the other hand, it would be hard, I
think, to pronounce my books as Christian novels unless you
were to go so far as to say that any novel that acknowledges
epistemological self-assurance to the point of permitting us
to say, "They're wrong and you're right," has got to be traced
to that sense of certitude that is distinctively Christian.

INTERVIEWER
Yes, you're certainly not *preaching* in the novels. Blackford
Oakes occasionally prays, which is just as natural to him as
breathing, but his Christianity doesn't color everything. I was
just wondering whether the Christians who write novels have
become an underground sect, as Christians were at the outset.

BUCKLEY
I think to a significant extent they have. Raymond Williams—the late British novelist—was the last novelist I can
think of offhand who was a flat-out Christian novelist. Am I
wrong?

INTERVIEWER
Frederick Buechner has been plying his trade as a Christian
novelist. George Garrett. His big novels are set in the Elizabe-
than era, but they're written with Christianity very much alive
and at issue. And, at times, include spies. I wonder if spying
and religion are in some way natural literary bedmates?

BUCKLEY
Well, isn't it safe to say that people who pursued the Communist objective—certainly early on—were motivated by
ideological convictions that were almost religious in nature?

Religious in the sense that they called for sacrifice and for the acceptance of historicism. That became less and less so as fewer and fewer people of moral intelligence actually believed in Leninism and communism. What they then believed in was Russian expansionism, and they became mere agents of the Soviet Union.

INTERVIEWER

So it began with religious fervor, which supplanted what traditional religion might have been for some.

BUCKLEY

I think so. These days it would be hard to find somebody in his twenties comparable to Whittaker Chambers in his twenties. This doesn't mean that there aren't still communists — Angela Davis is a very noisy communist, but she's shallow. There isn't really a sense of life in the catacombs, the kind of thing you had in the twenties and thirties, when people like Malcolm Muggeridge (until his early epiphany) were, temporarily, in thrall to the idea of the collectivist state.

INTERVIEWER

Do you think that in a time when the visible attachment of many people to formal religious institutions has been waning there has been a corresponding attraction to other causes?

BUCKLEY

Yes, I do. And for that reason it is not easy to command a large public. Most writers want a large public, and tend for that reason not to write religious novels. And explicitly religious — God, it's been so long since I've read one — an explicitly religious novel would be looked on merely as a period piece.

INTERVIEWER

How do you handle the technical stuff in the novel? Do you do your own research?

BUCKLEY

I am very unmechanical. I remember once, halfway through writing *Stained Glass*, I had to fly back to New York from Switzerland to do two or three episodes of *Firing Line* to catch up. I called my electrician in Stamford and I didn't have a lot of time; so I just said, "Could you please tell me how to execute somebody with electricity?" Well, he was sort of dumbfounded.

INTERVIEWER

He doesn't make house calls of that kind?

BUCKLEY

That's right. And he hadn't really given it much thought, he sort of muttered a couple of utterly unusable things like, "Put him in a bathtub and have him fix electricity." So I mentioned this in a letter to a historian at the University of San Jose. He wrote back and said, "I must introduce you to my friend, Alfred Aya." Aya turned out to be a bachelor, aged then about fifty-five, who worked for the telephone company. As my friend described him, at heart a physicist — and more. When he was six years old and traveled with his parents, he would inevitably disappear for four or five minutes in the hotel, and from that moment on anybody who pushed UP on the elevator went down, and anybody who pushed DOWN went up. Aya loves challenges. So I wrote him a letter and said, "Look, I've got this problem." He gave me the idea of executing him via this device, what I call a Chromoscope, which was entirely plausible. Later, he gave me all the information I needed to write satellite scenes in the later novel that dealt with the U-2, including how to make the thing appear to be coming down, and how to destroy it, et cetera. I remember when I came to the nuclear missile question — at this point we communicate with each other via E-mail because he's an E-mail nut, as am I — so I shot him a message via computer. Here's the problem: there's one nuclear weapon left in Cuba, and I have to know what it looks like. I must know what is needed to fire it, what is needed to redirect it to a target other than the one prescribed for it. And twenty-four hours later, I had a 29,000 word reply from him. Absolutely astonishing. Which made me, temporarily, one of the world's foremost authorities on how to handle a single nuclear bomb.

INTERVIEWER

Does he give you any credit for helping him work off aggressions?

BUCKLEY

He's absolutely delighted to help.

INTERVIEWER

What else is your system of research, since there is so much fact?

BUCKLEY

Wherever there is something concerning which I have a factual doubt, I put in a double parenthesis, which is a code to the librarian at *National Review*, who moonlights on my books, to check that, so she often will find five or six or seven hundred of those in the course of a novel. And she then copes.

INTERVIEWER

Are you aware of the category they now call the techno-thriller, like the novels of Tom Clancy and so on?

BUCKLEY

Well, I know Tom Clancy.

INTERVIEWER

I wonder whether these writers who make a fetish out of hardware have influenced you?

BUCKLEY

No, except that I admire it when it's done skillfully. For instance, Frederick Forsyth, in the book mentioned earlier, describes the assembly of the rifle with which he's going to attempt the assassination; I like the neatness with which he names the various parts. I have a book called *What's What*, in which you can look up *shoe* and find out exactly what you call this part of one, or that, etcetera.

INTERVIEWER

Now, famously, you write *everywhere*. You write in New York at *National Review*; you write in New York in your home; you write in Connecticut in your home; you write in the car; you write in planes; you write presumably in hotels. Is it only writing novels that is done in Switzerland?

BUCKLEY

In order not to break the rhythm, I almost always write a chapter on the airplane from Switzerland to here when I come back for my television work. Working on a novel, I like to write every day so as not to break it up. There are two nights when I cannot do it. Those are the nights when I am preparing for the television the following day. But I try not to miss more than two nights.

INTERVIEWER

Do you think when a novelist begins a novel, he has to live the novel, that you have to begin to become one or more of the characters, and you don't want to be interrupted playing those roles any more than an actor wants to be interrupted?

BUCKLEY

Oh, I am *feverishly* opposed to that idea. I've seen people wreck their lives trying to do it. I know the MacDowell Colony and Bread Loaf and such are pretty successful, but I also know that some people seclude themselves to write and become alcoholics precisely because they have nothing else to do. I have a close friend who has that problem, because when he sets out to write a novel, he wants to clear the decks. Nothing would drive me battier than to do *just* a novel over the course of an entire month. I have only *x* ergs of purely creative energy, and when I'm out of those, what in the hell do I do then?

When one sets out to write a book, I do believe one should attack it two or three hours a day, every day, without fail. You mustn't interrupt it to do a week's lecture tour or whatever. On the other hand, don't ever devote the entire day to doing just that, or the chances are you'll get bored with it, or simply run out of energy. But I'm glad you asked me that question, because I feel so strongly about it. I'd like to see more novels *not* written by people who have all the time in the world to write them.

INTERVIEWER

As an editor I spend half of my life trying to persuade people who think they should write books that they don't have to give up careers and certainly not family in order to write a book. They do have to find time — they have to make time — but they don't necessarily have to jump ship.

BUCKLEY

It seems so marvelous when you realize that and can say, "Look, fifteen hundred words a day," and you've got a book in six weeks.

INTERVIEWER

Now, when you wrote your first novel, I found it a surprise — an agreeable surprise — because I somehow thought it would be in homage to writers you liked.

BUCKLEY

Imitative? I don't have the skill to imitate. For instance, I admire people who can come up with a touch of a foreign accent. I just don't know how. There may be a school somewhere — Cornell? — that teaches you how to do that. And if I thought I could go somewhere for a half-day and learn how to make a character sound like a Spaniard, I would. My son has that skill, marvelously developed. I can't do it. I can't in

speaking either. I sometimes call somebody and don't want
to be recognized. But I don't know how to do it. And I don't
know how to write like anybody else.

INTERVIEWER

At the start, I didn't think you'd write a page-turner. I
thought, as I've said, that you would write a clever novel, an
intelligent novel, maybe ideologically weighted. What I didn't
see coming was the novel that moves ahead. I wonder if that
comes at least in part from the fact that you write quickly?

BUCKLEY

Well, perhaps in part. But mostly it's my terribly overdevel-
oped faculty against boredom. I was introduced into the White
House Fellows annual lunch affair by a man who had done
some research on my books, and he picked up a line I had
forgotten. "Mr. Buckley," he said, "has written that he gets
bored winding his watch." True, I was greatly relieved when
they developed the quartz. I never *just* brush my teeth, I'm
reading and brushing my teeth at the same time. So, if something bores me, then it's certainly going to bore somebody
else.

I live a hectic life. Someone once asked me if I ever could
lay aside my Christian scruples so as to have a mistress, and
I said, "I really don't have the time."

INTERVIEWER

You once said to me that you are not particularly reflective
or thoughtful. How can you write a novel with as many parts
and qualities, as many components, as many subplots and
themes as you do, and still say that you're not thoughtful,
not reflective?

BUCKLEY

Well, what that takes is hard concentration. I don't think
that people who are very busy are for that reason diluting the
attention that they give to what they are doing when they are

doing it. For instance, Churchill in his wonderful essay on painting said when he's painting that's *all* he's thinking about. When I'm painting, that's all I'm thinking about. I happen to be a lousy painter, I should admit instantly, but I enjoy it and I concentrate on it. Sometimes, going up in the lift with, say, Doris Brynner, a ski-mate, who's a wonderful listener, I'll say, "Now I've got to the point where I've got this problem, and this girl has to come out alive. On the other hand, she's going to be in the Lubyanka," that kind of thing—and just saying it helps. I only really think when I'm writing or talking. I suppose it's a gift of extemporaneity. But also, added to that method, I think is the usual one. When you reach a knotty problem in your novel, you sometimes have to sit back in your chair and think, "What am I going to do next?" I don't want to give the impression that I simply keep using my fingers.

INTERVIEWER

Reviewers have noticed, and it has always intrigued me, that you write your enemies so well that it sometimes seems as if you characterize them better than *our* guys—the good guys. Your portraits of Castro, of Che Guevara, of Khrushchev, Beria and so on, are all close, pores and all. . . .

BUCKLEY

Nobody can possibly like the Beria that I depicted.

INTERVIEWER

No, I don't mean it's necessary to *like* them, but you give them so much color. Blackford sometimes pales—and I suspect this is your intention—by comparison to the roster of heavies.

BUCKLEY

Well, exposure to these historical characters is almost always limited. In the first book in which Khrushchev appears, he makes, I think, two appearances. Therefore you take the essence of Khrushchev and give it to the reader, and the reader is grateful, because it *is* the essence of what we know or can imagine about him. If you had to write 450 pages about Khrushchev, you'd run the danger of etiolation. I think I've read enough about these characters to have some idea of what they're like. I depended heavily on Carlos Franke when I wrote about Castro and Che Guevara. Guevara was a very magnetic human being. Cruel, and entirely obsessed, but nevertheless attractive. Fidel Castro is more attractive to ten thousand people than he is to ten people, whereas Che Guevara was the other way around. I think I captured Castro well, but I'm equally pleased with the portraits I've drawn of Americans, the Dulles brothers and Dean Acheson.

INTERVIEWER

Let's speak for a moment of the amount you write and the presumed speed at which you write, novels and everything else. Do you have any models or inspirations who helped you to this sustained burst of intellectual and creative activity?

BUCKLEY

I'm not sure I'm all that fast or all that productive. Take for example, Trollope. He'd rise at five-thirty, do his toilette and have his breakfast, all by six. He would then begin writing, and he had a note pad that had been indexed to indicate intervals of 250 words. He would force himself to write 250 words per 15 minutes. Now, if at the end of 15 minutes he hadn't reached one of those little marks on his page, he would write faster. And if he passed the goal in 15 minutes he would write more slowly! And he wrote that way for three hours — 3,000 words a day.

INTERVIEWER

Do you approve?

BUCKLEY

If you were told to write a cantata every Sunday, and you got what Bach got out of it, how could you disapprove of it?

INTERVIEWER

Do you keep to a particular standard with your work?

BUCKLEY

It's true about everybody, that some stuff is better than other stuff. But I don't release anything that isn't, roughly speaking—I say *roughly* speaking—as good as it can be. If I reread, say, my column, a third time, I probably would make a couple of changes. I'm aware of people who create both, so to speak, the "quality stuff" and the "non-quality stuff," who think nothing of writing two or three pulp novels per year. Bernard DeVoto was that way. I can't do that, and I don't do that. I'm not sure I could. What I write—especially the books—needs a lot of work. So I always resent critics who find themselves saying, "Mr. Buckley's novels look as though they were written with one eye on the in-flight movie."

INTERVIEWER

Nobody's been clever enough to say that.

BUCKLEY

R.Z. Sheppard in *Time* magazine did. Who, by the way, has often praised my books. So it would be odd, I think, for someone who has reached age seventy, which I have, to write as much as I do without being able to discipline himself.

INTERVIEWER

Although you don't measure it out like Trollope, nevertheless you know you have so many days and weeks in February and March in which to write a novel.

BUCKLEY

Well, I'm much slower than Trollope . . . and never mind the differences in quality. If Trollope had given himself, say, six hours instead of three, would his novels have been that much better? I don't know that anybody could reach that conclusion. But then he took three hours to write three thousand words, which is very fast writing when using a pencil, but not fast at all when you're using a word processor.

It should change the statistics.

When I sit down to start writing every day in Switzerland, which is usually about a quarter to five to about seven fifteen — two and a half hours — it's inconceivable to me that I would write less than fifteen hundred words during that time. That's much slower than Trollope, even though I have faster tools. So, although I write fast, I'm not a phenomenally fast writer.

Speechwriters get told by the president that he's going to declare war the next day and to please draft an appropriate speech. And they do it. Or, Tom Wicker. I've seen him write ten thousand words following one day's trial proceedings, and all that stuff will appear in *The New York Times*. Now it's not belletrism, but it's good journalistic craftsmanship.

There's no automatic merit in being fast or slow. Whatever works, works. Georges Simenon, who was a phenomenon of production, always got himself in shape to write each novel. I hate to mention this in your presence, but he usually wrote his novels in seven or eight days. He had a physical beforehand, I think perhaps particularly for blood pressure, and then went into a kind of trance and wrote the novel, and then was ordered by his doctor to go off and take a vacation.

I'll go you one better. Rotzan Isagner, who does not go to sleep until he has finished the book.

Your workroom in Switzerland. What is that like?

BUCKLEY

Well, it's a converted children's playroom. I have my desk and my reference library at one end; there's the harpsichord and gramophone, and there's a Ping-Pong table on which all the paints are . . .

INTERVIEWER

Do you play music while you're writing? Do you write to Scarlatti, or to Bach, or . . .

BUCKLEY

Do I play? . . . Oh, my goodness! Heavens, yes! I thought you meant, did I play myself? Occasionally, I get up and— you know, in a moment of boredom or whatever—hit a few notes. But the answer is, yes, I have the record player on most of the time. Also, in Switzerland one of the better socialized institutions—but I love it—is that you can, for a few francs per month, attach to your telephone a little music-box device which gives you six channels, one of them a good music channel.

INTERVIEWER

Is there any link between what you're writing and what you're listening to?

BUCKLEY

No, none whatever.

INTERVIEWER

So you could play Fats Waller one time and Beethoven another?

BUCKLEY

I don't play jazz when I write. I don't know why but I just plain don't. But I do when I paint.

INTERVIEWER

What about revising?

BUCKLEY
Of all the work I do, it's the work I look forward to most—rewriting. I genuinely, *genuinely* enjoy that, especially with the invention of the word processor, which makes it mechanically so neat.

INTERVIEWER
So partly it's the technological joy of working with these instruments?

BUCKLEY
Yes.

INTERVIEWER
You've said more than once that you find writing is hard work.

BUCKLEY
But how would the reader know? Writing, if it's done at all, has got to yield net satisfaction. But that satisfaction is long after the foreplay. I'm not saying that I wish I were otherwise engaged professionally. I'm simply saying that writing is terribly hard work. But it doesn't follow at all that because it's hard work, it's odd that it's done so quickly. I think that's quite natural. If writing is pain, which it is to me, it should follow that the more painful the exercise is, the more quickly you want to get on with it. The obvious analogy, I suppose, would be an execution. For years they've been trying to figure out how to execute a person more quickly, so that he feels less protracted pain. That's a *reductio ad absurdum*. In any event, if your living depends on writing a piece of journalism every day, and you find writing painful work, you're obviously much better off developing the facility to execute it in an hour rather than ten hours.

INTERVIEWER
You're a computer maven, you've been through all the known stages of man with regard to writing and its instru-

ments. You presumably started writing by hand or, as some people would insist, with a quill pen, yes?

BUCKLEY

Well, I did in this sense: until I was writing every day for the *Yale Daily News*, as its editor, I would write by hand and then type, so the typewritten copy would be draft number two. It happens that my handwriting is sort of malformed. In fact, my father, when I was fifteen years old, sent me a typewriter with the instructions: learn to use it, and never write to him in longhand again. So I learned the touch-type system, and by the time I was twenty-three it wouldn't occur to me to write anything by hand. In fact, I was so unhappy doing so that I would ask my professors' permission, on the honor system, to type an exam instead of writing it. And with one exception, they all said sure. I'd take one of those blue books into the next room and type away.

INTERVIEWER

About vocabulary: you get criticized, or satirized, for your use of arcane words. Are you conscious of reining in your vocabulary when you're writing a novel?

BUCKLEY

No, I don't think I am. In the novels, there's less obvious analysis than in nonfiction work. I'm attached to the conviction that sometimes the word that you want has an in-built rhythm that's useful. And there are some words that are onomatopoeic, and when they are, they too can be very useful. Let me give you a concrete example. This morning, I wrote about Arafat's speech, and the coverage of the speech, which consumed most of the television news last night. This had to do with the question: did he or did he not live up to the demands of the State Department that he denounce violence absolutely, agree to abide by the relevant resolutions of the United Nations Security Council and acknowledge the existence of Israel? Now, all the commentators said he skirted the subject, that his language was sometimes ambiguous. I concluded that he had more nearly consummated his inherent pledge — "however *anfractuous* the language." Now the word came to me not only as a useful word but also as a necessary word. I first ran into that word in a review by Dwight MacDonald of Norman Mailer's book on the Pentagon, *The Armies of the Night*, and I didn't know what it meant; I couldn't figure it out by internal inspection, so I looked it up. And that's *exactly* the word to describe Arafat's discussion of Israel's existence. There is an example of where one could use *ambiguous*, but that extra syllable makes it sound just a little bit more "windy."

I remember once in a debate with Gore Vidal at which David Susskind was deriding me in San Francisco, 1964, I used the word *irenic*, which didn't disturb Vidal, of course. So after it was over, Susskind said, "What's *irenic?*" I said, "Well, you know, sort of serene, sort of peaceful." "Well, why didn't you say serene or peaceful?" And I said, "Because the other word is a better fit." At this point believe it or not, Vidal, who was on Susskind's side a hundred percent during the exchange, said, "You know the trouble with you, David, is that you don't learn anything, ever."

INTERVIEWER

Irenic is a nice word.

BUCKLEY

And again onomatopoeic. So, in defending the use of these words, I begin by asking the question: why were they invented? They must have been invented because there was, as the economist put it, "a felt need" for them. That is to say, there came a moment at which a writer felt that the existing inventory didn't quite do what he wanted it to do. These words were originally used because somebody with a sensitive ear felt the need for them. Do you therefore, because it's very seldom that one hears an A-flat diminished tenth, say to yourself, I won't use that chord, notwithstanding the pleasure it gives to people whose ears are educated enough to hear that little difference? People don't say to a musician, please don't use any unusual chords.

Anfractuous is a more vigorous, almost violent word.

Yes, it suggests a little hint of the serpentine, a little bit of the impenetrable going around and around. So therefore why not use it? Years ago, the review of *God & Man at Yale*, again by *Time* magazine, referred to my "apopemptic" book on leaving Yale. So, of course I looked it up, because I didn't know what it meant, and it's different from *valedictorian*, because an apopemptic speech, if memory serves, is usually what the ruler gives to the pilgrims en route somewhere. His sort of final message and advice. So the writer on *Time*, whoever he was in 1951, was making a very shrewd difference between *valedictory*—I'm leaving Yale—and giving Yale my parting advice; in effect, *Time* set me up as if I were the ruler of Yale, giving my subjects my advice. Very nice. So occasionally I use *apopemptic*, and when I use it, it's strictly when I want that tiny little difference in inflection, which is worth making.

You once said you use the words you know.

A good point. Everybody knows words that other people don't know. Reading *The Coup*, I found twenty-six words in it I didn't know. I listed them in a column, and there were great hoots in my office because everybody knew quite a lot of them. So we went around the table—there were, you know, eight or ten editors, including James Burnham—and by the time we got all the way around, all twenty-six, there was, as I say, much jollity over that.

INTERVIEWER

So words are put into your vocabulary by other writers?

BUCKLEY

Yes. I'm offended by people who suggest—and some
have—that I spend my evenings with dictionaries. I'm reminded that in his wonderful review of *Webster's Third*,
Dwight MacDonald referred to "words that belong in the zoo-
pages of the dictionary." There are certain words that I couldn't
bring myself to use, not because they aren't instrumentally
useful, but because they just look too inventionistic. How they
got there, one never quite knows. A lot of them are sort of
medical.

INTERVIEWER

So, for those who might have thought your use of language
elitist, you have quite the reverse view. You trust your reader
to either know it, or look it up, or go over it like a smooth
ski jump.

BUCKLEY

The reader can say, "I don't care, it's not worth my time."
But there's no reason why he should deprive other people
grateful for that tenth augmented chord, which gives them
pleasure. Did you know that forty percent of the words used
by Shakespeare were used by him only once? I've never read
a satisfactory explanation of the seventeenth-century capacity
to understand the stuff we hear with some sense of strain.
Shakespeare used a total of twenty-eight thousand words, most
of them were within reach of the audience. And when you
consider that books by Cardinal Newman were serialized as
recently as a hundred years ago. *The Apologia* was serialized
and upped the circulation of a London daily. Imagine serializ-
ing *The Apologia* today. Or take the difference between a
Lincoln-Douglas debate and a Kennedy-Nixon debate . . .
Lincoln, in that rich, biblical vocabulary of his, was not at all
self-conscious about using a wide vocabulary.

I've never seen a test, though I'd like to see it done, that would scan say three or four pages of the current issue of *The New York Times* and three or four pages of a hundred years ago of, say, the *Tribune*, and find out what the so-called Fog Index reveals.

INTERVIEWER

The Fog Index?

BUCKLEY

The Fog Index is the average number of syllables per word and the average number of words per sentence.

INTERVIEWER

In writing fiction, your vocabulary is nevertheless somewhat constrained by the fact that you are limited to the words that your characters would use?

BUCKLEY

Absolutely. Except that one of my characters is a Ph.D., and I remember on one occasion she used the word *syllepsis*. Christopher Lehmann-Haupt wrote, "Mr. Buckley's character doesn't even know how correctly to use the word *syllepsis*; she really meant . . ." Anyway, he gave me a wonderful opportunity, since a second printing was coming out right away, to go back and rewrite the dialogue to have her say, "*Syllepsis* — a word the correct meaning of which is not even acknowledged by the *New York Times* critics."

INTERVIEWER

To shift a bit, in a conversation with Louis Auchincloss, you asked why people take less satisfaction from novels than they used to.

BUCKLEY

Well, I mentioned television as the principal time-consumer, and it just plain is. It's been established statistically that the average American has the television set turned on between thirty-five and thirty-nine hours per week.

If people derive fewer rewards from novels than they used to, does this reflect something about the novels themselves, rather than the competition for time?

Well, it certainly can. It can also suggest that the passive intelligence is less resourceful than it used to be. My favorite book at age nine was called *The Magic of Oz*. If you could correctly pronounce a string of consonants, you could turn yourself into a giraffe. I can't imagine a nine-year-old today being engrossed — being *diverted*, let alone being engrossed — by that because he would want to see it happening on the screen.

He'd want to see dancing consonants.

That's right.

People have traditionally turned to novels, at least some, for a way to get a grip on the world, a way to see the order in the chaos. Have we gone past that period? Is it that many novels are not so avidly consumed because they provide small delights, rather than provide epiphanies, or grand epiphanies?

I think reading the many contemporary novels you get some of that feeling of, "Where in the hell have I been that it was worthwhile going to?"

People often think you are writing about yourself in the Blackford Oakes novels.

Of course, it becomes very easy if one takes the obvious profile. You begin with the fact that we were both born the same year and went to Yale at approximately the same time. Now, I made him a Yale graduate—I think it was the class of 1951—for sheer reasons of personal sloth. I was in the class of 1950, so I knew that I could coast on my knowledge of the scene without having to go and visit a fresh college and see how things happened there. Then, for the same reason, i.e., sloth, I made him an undercover agent of the CIA, so that I could give him the identical training I had received and know that it was absolutely legitimate. So that much was, if you like, autobiographical . . . if you can say it's autobiographical that two different people went to Yale and to the CIA, and spend time describing Yale and the CIA. But beyond that, people who want to sustain the parallel have a tough time. In the first place he's an engineer, a Protestant. He has a sweetheart whom he has yet to marry—I married when I was twenty-four years old. He's a pilot, which I was not. He signed up in the CIA as a *profession*, which I didn't. I knew I was only going to be temporary and I'd quit after nine months. He's not a writer. There's a little touch of James Bond in his experiences, which there never was in mine, which were very sedentary. To be sure, it is quite true that he's conservative. In fact, for the fun of it I have him read *National Review* and occasionally read stuff of mine and Whittaker Chambers and so on. And he's also pro-American. And we're both bright, sure.

And you're both admirers of Bill Buckley.

Exactly! Though sometimes he kind of lags behind a little bit. Should I tell my favorite story about the reviewer in Kansas

City? He reviewed *Saving the Queen* for *The Kansas City Star*, and he had obviously spent much of his adult life abominating everything I had ever done, said or written. But he didn't quite dislike the novel, and this terribly disturbed him. He got over it with his final line. He said, "The protagonist of *Saving the Queen* is tall, handsome, endearing, engaging, compassionate, amusing—from which at least we have the satisfaction of knowing that the book was not autobiographical." Nice line.

INTERVIEWER

About Blackford Oakes again: there are some disagreements about your style. Just running barefoot through some of these critical notices, I see: "Oakes is as bloodless as well-done English roast beef,"—that's a reviewer in Florida—vs. Anatole Broyard in *The New York Times*: "In every respect he is a welcome relief from the unromantic superiority and disengagement of a James Bond. Beneath this Cold War there beats a warm heart." Then we get from another reviewer: "Blackie has a distinctive personality"—and from another lines like: "A flat character and an annoying name-dropper." You attract lines like: "A Rambo with a Yale degree," and all sorts of things. This character of yours seems to be capable of stirring up a lot of confusing and conflicting opinions. Maybe that's biographical.

BUCKLEY

Well, yes, I have a feeling—I hate to say it—but I have a feeling this is mostly a confusion of things about me. I simply decline to believe that two or three of those things said about Blackford Oakes would have been said if the books had been written by Mary Gordon, say. They just wouldn't have said it, and they wouldn't have *thought* it. Now, whether they convinced themselves that this was so, or whether they feel the stereotypical compulsion to say it must be so because I wrote it, I don't know. I've never asked anybody. I'd like to think that Anatole Broyard is not easily seduced—at least not by me — and I like to think that Blackford Oakes is an interesting human being. True, in certain of the novels he plays a relatively minor and flat role. But never quite as minor as people have sometimes charged.

INTERVIEWER

You seem to attract reviews that don't have much to do with the book at hand.

BUCKLEY

My son Christopher thinks I suffer from overexposure, and I'm sure he's right. I'd like to think some of my books would have done better if they had been published under an assumed name, so that people wouldn't feel they had to do the Buckley bit before talking about the book. It's especially true in England, by the way, although I'm underexposed in England in the sense that I'm not all over the place. Some aspects of my situation as a novelist are probably unique. Gore Vidal is very public in his experiences, but he's episodic. He goes away for a year and a half — thank God — and then he writes his book and then he comes back and publicizes it. Norman Mailer, during his *Village Voice* period, and right after, was almost always in the news, not for something he had said or for a position he had taken, about which people ceased caring, but for something he had done. You know, urinated in the Pentagon, or married his seventh wife or got drunk at his fiftieth birthday, that kind of thing. But I assault the public three times a week in the column and once a week on television, and every fortnight if they elect to read the *National Review*. So that's kind of a hard battering ram for people disposed to be impatient, either as critics or as consumers, with a novel written by me.

INTERVIEWER

That puts your critics to a particular test, that is, to detach themselves.

BUCKLEY

Anatole Broyard was very attentive and receptive, and so was Lehmann-Haupt. Between them they've reviewed almost everything I've written.

INTERVIEWER

Did you say once that when you decided to write a novel John Braine sent you a book on how to write one?

BUCKLEY

We were friends. John Braine was born again, politically. This was along around 1957 or 1958, when he ceased to be an angry young man and became an early deplorer of the excesses with which we became familiar in the 1960s and 1970s. So he used to write me regularly, and I had lunch with him once or twice in London; he was on my television program, along with Kingsley Amis. But then he . . . he was a little bit moody and he sort of stopped writing his letters. There wasn't any implicit act of hostility, I just had the feeling he wasn't writing his twenty-five people per week, that kind of thing. But when I sent him a letter saying that I was going to write a novel, he said, "Well, I wrote a book on how to write a novel, and here it is." So I read it.

INTERVIEWER

Was it helpful?

BUCKLEY

I remember only one thing — which doesn't mean that I wasn't influenced by a hundred things in it — but he said that the reading public expects one coincidence and is cheated if it isn't given one, but scorns two.

INTERVIEWER

Have you written a lot about other authors?

BUCKLEY

Not a lot, some. A lot of authors have been on *Firing Line*.

I remember Borges especially.

He was stupendous. He was living in Buenos Aires. I had lunched with him a few years earlier, in Boston, while he was visiting professor at Harvard. A friend—Herbert Kenny, then the literary editor of *The Boston Globe*—had brought us together. Borges was already blind. He did not mind it, he said, because now he could "live his dreams with less distraction."

Then we met in Buenos Aires, in 1977, during the military junta days. He seemed astonishingly frail, but he spoke without a pause. I remember thinking of Nabokov, who told me he couldn't come on *Firing Line* because he would need to memorize everything he would then say. I said, come on, your extemporaneous talk is absolutely lapidary. He said no, he had never spoken in public in his entire life, including lectures to students, without first memorizing what he would say.

Anyway, Borges was like that. I didn't interrupt him. I remember beginning by asking whether he thought of himself as in the company of other blind poets, Homer and Milton. Here is what he says, I'll give it to you from my book *On the Firing Line*. He said . . . "Of course, when you are blind, time flows in a different way. It flows, let's say, on an easy slope. I have sometimes spent sleepless nights—night before last, for example—but I didn't really feel especially unhappy about it, because time was sliding down that—was flowing down."

I asked him how he refreshed himself, as a blind man. "I'm reading all the time. I'm having books reread to me. I do very little contemporary reading. But I'm only going back to certain writers, and among those writers I would like to mention an American writer. I would like to mention Emerson. I think of Emerson not only as a great prose writer—everybody knows that—but as a very fine intellectual poet, as the only intellectual poet who had any *ideas*. Emerson was brimming over with ideas." We talked about Emerson a bit and then I said, "Who else?" He mentioned Hawthorne but came in with a qualification right away. "What I dislike about Hawthorne is,

he was always writing fables. In the case of Poe, well, you get
tales; but there is no moral tagged on to them." He didn't
linger but went to Melville. "But I think of Melville, one of
the great writers of the world, no?"

I agreed. I asked him then—I'm looking at my book, since
my memory, on its own, couldn't re-track this way, though
Borges' certainly could—why he chose to be unfamiliar with
new writers.

"I am afraid that I'd find the new writers more or less like
myself." I'm glad I had the wit to comment, "You won't."

But what really got me was his handling of language. Listen:
"I have no Greek, but I had Latin. Of course, my Latin is very
rusty. But still, as I once wrote, to have forgotten Latin is
already, in itself, a gift. To have known Latin and to have
forgotten it is something that sticks to you somehow. I have
done most of my reading in English. I read very little in Spanish. I was educated practically in my father's library, and that
was compounded of English books. So that when I think of
the bible, I think of the King James Bible. When I think of
the *Arabian Nights*, I think of Lane's translation, or of Captain
Burton's translation. When I think of Persian literature, I think
in terms of Browne's *Literary History of Persia*, and of course
of Fitzgerald's. And, frankly, I remember the first book I read
on the history of South America was Prescott's *The History
of the Conquest of Peru*."

We contrasted English and Spanish, and why he considered
English a far finer language than Spanish—during which, I
might add, he did a little cadenza in German, which he taught
himself so he could read Schopenhauer in the original. Then
I asked him if the fact that the Spanish language is less resourceful than the English language necessarily makes it less
complete as poetry. He replied, "No. I think that when poetry
is achieved, it can be achieved in *any* language. It's more that
a fine Spanish verse that could hardly be translated to another
language would turn to something else. But when *beauty*
happens, well, there it is. No?

"What Whistler said—people were discussing art in Paris,
about the influence of *heredity*, *tradition*, *environment* and

so on — was in his lazy way, 'Art happens.' 'Art *happens*,' he said. And I think that's true. I should say that *beauty* happens.

"Sometimes I think that beauty is not something rare. I think beauty is happening *all* the time. *Art* is happening all the time. At some conversation a man may say a very fine thing, not being aware of it. I am hearing fine sentences all the time from the man in the street, for example. From anybody."

I asked him if he considered himself a transcriber, to a certain extent. He said, "Yes, in a sense I do, and I think that I have written some fine lines, of course. *Everybody* has written some fine lines. That's not *my* privilege. If you're a writer you're bound to write something fine, at least now and then, off and on."

I brought up Longfellow. "Longfellow has some very beautiful lines. I'm very old-fashioned, but I like, 'This is the forest primeval. The murmuring pines and the hemlocks.' That's a very fine line. I don't know why people look down on Longfellow."

I asked him if in his experience it was possible to stimulate a love of literature. Was it possible to take twenty people and make them love literature more? He replied, "I'd been a professor of English and American literature during some twenty years, at the University of Buenos Aires. And I tried to teach my students not literature — that can't be taught — but the love of literature. If the course has to be done in four months, I can do very little. But still I know there are many young men in Buenos Aires — maybe they're not so young now — young men and young women, who have their memories full of English verse. And I have been studying Old English and Old Norse for the last twenty years. And I have also taught many people the love of Old English. I find something very stirring about Old English poetry."

I asked, "It has to stand on its own two feet, you mean?" Borges replied, "It has to. Or maybe because I like the sound of it. 'Maeg ic be my sylfum sothgied wrecan, / Sithas secgan' — now, those sounds have a *ring* to them. They mean, 'I can utter a true song about myself. I can tell of my travels.' That sounds like Walt Whitman, no? That was written in the ninth century in Northumberland. 'Maeg ic be me sylfum sothgied wrecan, / Sithas secgan' — and Ezra translated it as this (I think it's a rather uncouth translation): 'May I for my own self song's truth reckon, / Journey's jargon.' Well, that's too much of a jargon to *me*, no? Of course, he's translating the sounds. 'Maeg ic be me sylfum sothgied wrecan, / Sithas secgan / — 'May I for my sake song's truth reckon,' — 'sothgied wrecan.' He's translating the sounds more than the sense. And then 'sithas secgan' — 'tell of my travels' — he translates 'journey's jargon,' which is rather uncouth, at least to me."

I asked him — after all, he'd said Pound's was uncouth — how he would have translated it. He replied, "I would translate it literally. 'I can utter, I can say a true song about myself. I can tell my travels.' I think that should be enough."

INTERVIEWER

You obviously enjoyed him.

BUCKLEY

I wrote in my book that his was the outstanding show. But I'd better stop here, though he went on, in his magic way.

INTERVIEWER

Is there anyone or anything you would never write about?

BUCKLEY

I wouldn't write anything that I was simply not at home with. I wouldn't write a western novel, for instance. I'm not sure I'd want to write *Advise and Consent* — the inside-the-Senate type of novel.

INTERVIEWER

Why don't you think about writing a novel like Tom Wolfe's — the novel of manners, of certain strata of society, of the mixture of social and political and business life. You have the keen observer's eye, and maybe not quite the same rapier instinct that Tom has for the false note, and . . .

BUCKLEY

And certainly not his descriptive powers, nor his talent for caricature. Because those are indispensable weapons. For the first few chapters of *Bonfire of the Vanities*, I underlined just his descriptions of people's clothes, and in a million years I couldn't achieve that.

INTERVIEWER

It's true, there are no caricatures in your novels that I can think of, tempting as it must have been to do so with some of the darker figures.

BUCKLEY

Well, some people thought the queen was. I didn't think so. I thought she was a somewhat Dickensian, original creation. I'm really quite serious. The fact that she's terribly sharp-tongued and terribly sarcastic, terribly aware of the fact that she's nominally sovereign and actually powerless, I think adds to the credibility of her character. I would love to see her on the stage. As done by Bette Davis.

INTERVIEWER

It's amusing to think back on how difficult it was for your agents to find publication in England for *Saving the Queen* because of your sacrilege in having Blackford Oakes bed down with her, even though a fictional queen.

BUCKLEY

And I have no doubt that not only killed that book in England, but probably inhibited its successors also.

INTERVIEWER

Have the novels been any kind of turning point? What have they meant to you? I have a feeling you took on the first one as a challenge—you wanted to test yourself against the form and have some fun, which you certainly did—and then?

BUCKLEY

I did find that there were reserves of creative energy that I was simply unaware of. Obviously, as a nonfiction analyst, one has to think resourcefully, but if, let's say in the novel I'm depicting a Soviet prison train going from Moscow to Siberia. I've got to create something that can hold the reader's attention during that journey. The answer became: you can do that. And it's kind of nice to figure out that you *can* do that . . . create a story that carries you from there.

— **Sam Vaughan**

Two Stories
by
Ben Sonnenberg

Recherché

"Do you know Portofino?" the Frenchman said.

"I was there once," the young man said.

"Portofino is splendid."

"I didn't like it that much."

"Portofino is splendid."

"Too many tourists, too many cars—"

The young man called to the waiter and ordered a second *café crème*. The waiter looked at the Frenchman. The Frenchman waved his hand no.

"Portofino is splendid." The Frenchman, who wore a button of the Légion d'honneur in his lapel, lit an American cigarette. "*If* you have a yacht.

The young man said he did not have a yacht.

"With a yacht," the Frenchman said, "I can be in Monte

in half an hour, in Saint-Tropez, in Cap d'Antibes . . ." He gave the young man a gracious wave of well-to-do abandon, as if leaving him behind on the dock. "I can step on shore — dark glasses, straw hat, a ten-thousand franc note in my pocket — *et voilà*, no one knows who I am."

A black Citroën pulled up to the curb and the Frenchman was sped away. The young man savored his feelings of inferiority. How delicious to be in Paris, to be lonely, to be scorned. The young man lit a French cigarette. That "*Et voilà*, no one knows who I am"! . . . The young man took out his fountain pen and wrote in a spiral notebook: "Only a wealthy Frenchman could have pronounced so *recherché* a desire for anonymity."

He felt very proud of that sentence. His literary idols were Marcel Proust and Thomas Mann. In the spiral notebook, on the front of which was written Paris 1955, the young man turned back a few pages and read:

> Gloucester, Mass. I am fourteen. Mommy's friend, the composer S.M.L.B., tells me I have "an Italian chin and Moroccan eyes." His own eyes are on my bare legs. I pretend I don't know what he means. He says, "I have slept with just about everything, including that cat." I give S. a blank look and bend over to peer at the cat. S. can see the crack of my butt. I stand up and turn and face him. He says, "A boy's first virginity is in his mouth."
>
> I lose my second virginity on my second night in Paris. I am twenty-two.
>
> Must read Baudelaire and Rimbaud. Also Jean Genet?

At that moment a middle-aged couple walked by, "Aren't you Arthur?" the woman exclaimed. "Look, Harry," she said to her husband. "Arthur!"

"Why, so it is!" said Harry. "Arthur, don't you recognize us?"

The young man knew who they were alright: Harry and Sylvia Rubin, friends of his parents, from New York. They lived at 812 Park Avenue and collected abstract expressionist art.

The woman said again, "Arthur?"

Arthur Freed got up abruptly and threw down on the table a handful of one-hundred franc notes. "*Pardon*," he said, "*je ne parle pas anglais.*"

The Crease

For Padgett Powell

He was in the bathtub when she came in and when he got out he went into the bedroom and started putting on his shorts. "I have lost all respect for you," she said.

"Isn't it about time?"

"You must have known I'd find out."

"You know I don't like showdowns."

"Were there others?" she said.

"Look here—" he said.

"I want you to tell me."

He picked out a shirt.

"I want *you* to tell me," she said again.

And so he told her. While getting dressed he listed a number of women, including an underground actress who lived in the same hotel. "Brought her baby with her," he added and grinned.

Her last words to him were, to his surprise, "Wasn't *that* cavalier."

After she left, he knotted his tie and made a cold face in the mirror. A short affair remarkable for her sweetness, his sharpness and its abrupt end. An affair much shorter to him than to her, he was certain of that. She would be obsessed with him for a time, calling him up at all hours, following him at night . . . Still, the affair had been long enough to include summer weekends with her wealthy Connecticut family, much going out as a couple, a planned trip to the south of France, as well as an abortion.

Now that it was over, he keenly felt: a sour sort of pride.

●

Soon after that he got married and soon after that he left his wife. And soon after that he conveniently moved into the young girl's apartment, on Hudson Street in the Village. She let him store his belongings there and use her car whenever he liked.

They went out a lot as a couple again. People who saw them together were frightened for her and if they knew her, they told her. This time he and she were planning a trip to Turkey and Greece.

One night, with another couple, they went to a restaurant for dinner, Downey's on Eighth Avenue. The restaurant was crowded and noisy. The women were still at the table and the two men were walking out when she distinctly heard him say, over all of the laughter and chatter and din, "Do you happen to know an apartment where I could take Kate for the night?"

"I never said that," he said in the car.

"I heard you distinctly."

"I don't believe it." Truly, he was incredulous. "Downey's was just too noisy."

"I'm telling you," she said. "And I'll tell you something else." They were parked in front of his parents' house on Gramercy Park. "My boyfriend before you—"

"Spare me," he said.

But she didn't, she wouldn't.

●

At her place the following morning he told her he was sorry. They were eating biscuits and drinking tea. "I didn't want you to hear it that way. But the fact is, I've decided that I'm going to Greece with Kate."

At lunch he told Kate what happened next. "She threw hot tea on my trousers. Took the crease out of them. Look," he said. He stood up, he sat down. Then he said to Kate, "Serves me right, I suppose."

Carolyn Kizer

Anniversaries: Claremont Avenue, from 1945

I'm sitting on a bench at One Hundred and Fifteenth
and Riverside Drive, with my books beside me,
early for my lesson in Chinese
at Twenty-one Claremont, right around the corner.
Two little girls pass in front of me
wheeling a doll carriage, fussing
with the doll and the doll blanket: then casually
one of them says, "The president is dead,"
pulling the coverlet over the doll's head.
The other replies in a flat little voice, "Yes,
the president is dead." I think, "Strange children
who toy with the notion of mortality."

Wind sweeps from the Hudson. Chill. It's time to go.
In the lobby I press the button for the elevator;
at last it clanks to a stop, the doors slide open
and I confront the seamed black face of Joe
runneled with tears. So I know it's true:
the president is dead. We rise in silence
past the floor where a lonely boy may play
those holidays when he's freed from boarding school.
Thirty years later, almost to the day
I'll marry him, in a church eight blocks away.

The elevator groans to the fifth floor.
Bliss, the gentle Chinese wife, opens the door,
her smile faint in the lotus of her face.
My teacher, Chen, expressionless. We start the lesson
as if nothing unusual had occurred,
then fall silent. Bliss brings the balm of tea,
exquisite Bliss who, ten years further on

will hang herself in their pale blue bedroom
with one of Chen's ties.
Before our tea is cool my mother comes
smiling and weeping. Though the president and she
are of an age, like Bliss and me
she has lost the father
who'd almost seen us through a war.

When Mother and I take the Seventh Avenue subway
the cars are stuffed with people black and white;
strangers murmur to strangers, strangers crying
as they clutch their papers, headlines black on white.
There's comfort here, but it's cold as we straggle out
in the dark, to Sheridan Square.
Later my first sister-in-law will tell me
that at Vassar, girls were dancing on the tables
cheering the news—an alien breed.
I'm glad I wasn't there
but with the bereaved on Seventh Avenue.

In the eighties we go to stay with my husband's mother,
this cultivated student of art history
and liturgical music. She is a baseball nut
comparing notes with Joe as they watch TV.
Chen, who is friends with no one, reappears
in the Claremont lobby, after thirty years
and invites us for a drink.
As the elevator labors up I am suffused
with memories of Bliss: Bliss and her taste:
celadon walls, peach-blossom silk embroidery,
jade objects on the tables, jade
on her wrists, a flower at her throat,
that porcelain throat . . .
Bliss and your incense, your pleading tremulous heart.

At six, Chen answers the bell
and we step into a cavern grim as hell:

bare boards, a cot with dirty sheets,
card table, metal folding chair—and that is all.
In great gray swags, wallpaper peels from the walls,
a stack of *Wall Street Journals* in the corner.
Where are the carpets, the bibelots, the scrolls?
All gone, sold or destroyed. A bottle of whiskey
and three tumblers sit on the rickety table.
Miserable, we stand awkwardly and drink
while Chen tells us he's gambled it all away;
matter-of-factly says what we don't care to hear:
how in their final years Bliss and he
could only masturbate each other.
I bless my husband's upright stone-faced mother.

It's 1985: in pain, my mother-in-law has died.
Appraisers from Doyle pick through her possessions:
old furniture blistered by sun and central heat.
Twenty-one Claremont is no longer ours.
Recollections are blistered and faded too:
My husband's boyhood toys, my fragments of Chinese.
Mothers have disappeared. Wars come and go.
The past is present: what we choose to keep
by a process none of us can ever know.
Now those little girls are grandmothers
who must remember, after fifty years
the doll, the chill, the tears.
Greatness felled at a blow.
Memory fractured. Black and white apart.
No sense of direction, we Americans.
No place to go.

Two Poems by Philip Hodgins

The Last Few Days and Nights

So weakened by life he could just pass
through the world this hospital bed,
he lies as still as someone already dead.
Hi-tech machines surround him now like family.

Three floors below him lies the mortuary.
People there have been cleaned of their identity.
Impossible to tell who wore the business suits,
the pilot's uniform or the comfortable shorts.

A nurse comes in to tend to the machines.
Reaching across him to one of them her breast,
the left one, is momentarily pressed
into his face with pillow pressure softness.

He opens his eyes as if to some memory.
She gives him a look as intimate as surgery.

Home Is Where the Hurt Is

These days I take my dying seriously,
after trying, and failing, to make it into a joke.
The silence was what doomed me ultimately:
all those nervous efforts to provoke

a set response, anything to keep the flights
of fancy going no matter how insincere.
I was like an actor blinded by the footlights,
not sure if an audience is really there.

Now I'm living out the whole thing in my mind.
Not death itself, the overwhelming fact
of nonexistence, but that moment when we find
a link between our life and death, the final act.

Each connection is lived through, then undone.
Happy. Sad. Sacred. Scared. Every day a different one.

Two Poems by Alan Shapiro

Dream of the Dead

Not the tired figures of our own fatigue,
our misplaced envy, sleep eternal, peace
in the blank heaven of complete belonging.

Not steam on the hot pavement after rain,
the garbled rumors of a shape, a gesture
shy of the light, their gauzy shiftingness

itself too much confinement as each blurred
strand twists back in an agony of yearning
toward the mere dispersal they had risen from.

No, when the dead rose up before me, they,
the most recent dead as dead as the most ancient,
were the soul of fire without anything to burn,

hunger shorn of mouth, except the mouth,
the tinder, that our flesh provided, yours
and mine, for you and I were there, our naked

bodies now their entrance to a loved
estrangement, and as we began to move
together unaware, as the moistened skin

tensed slowly toward the sudden spasm, on
our vagrant lips, our curious fingers, over
every inch of us they burned and fed.

Pleasure

Ever obliging, faithful, good parents that they are,
when he's happiest, in his happy bed, his wife against him,
they call to him, his tutelary spirits of a moment
hidden now inside his pleasure, as his pleasure's underground.
They call, and the rapt eclipse, the mutual gasp and cry,
is suddenly the golden bough leading him back down stairs,
a child again, to the doorway where his mother stumbles,
yelling something, with her arms held like a shield before her
as his father swings, — just that, and nothing else beyond it,
no before, no after, and no terror either but the terror
of remembering that he was thrilled, not terrified at all,
as if they knew what would please him before he did himself,
tightening all along the coil of what he didn't know
was there, of what they hid from him so he would feel
only the sheer pleasure of its fierce release.
It was their first, their clearest lesson in fulfillment.
Ever after only the tantalizing substitutes, the sulks
and silences, the spectral pantomines, that left him
more expectant, hungry, dreaming the ever more vivid
dream of what they wouldn't do, withheld, he realizes now,
so he'd always want that pleasure, know how incomparable
    it was.
Here, where he's happiest, with his wife beside him, his hand
no heavier than breath along her arm and shoulder, they bring
him back to that original event because they love him, flesh
of their flesh, they want him to have everything they had.

John Voiklis

The Princeling's Apology

1

Where are my robes, my sword, the minted coins
inscribed *Pros Doxan* . . .? I ascend my throne.
When the Bishop, bearing unction, comes
to bless me, who will weave the laurel wreaths?

The Princess? Isn't that her ship that sails
toward another—dowry of peace on board?
Where is my cabinet? With state affairs
in shambles now, I need their prudent words.

Is that my loving nation: liar, thief,
traitor, milling through the streets? O God—
without a scarf, a ring, a basil sprig
behind my ear—my God, I am exposed.

2

The first—forgiven. Scolding now, when sin's
unknown, only compounds what's best snuffed out;
what first burned just the cheek inflames the skin:
fever thrums through temples, clenches throat,
drains lips. Relief requires I sin again.

3

Summer, Love, though not yet ripe, is rotten:
rent to pay and weather too severe.
Still, one hope remains; I haven't forgotten
the grocer's shipment of exotic fruit.
Anxious that my favorite's almost here,
I prowl the ships arriving at the pier
from Mexico, or farther off, Beirut.

Peeling back the purpling skin, I'll know
again that darkest flesh, enough to sate
my year-long appetite. Till then I'll gnaw
fingernails and tongue, hoping to earn
one taste. No matter how I salivate,
August to August, fasting, I await
the season's slow but imminent return.

4

Before the word, was breath: expanding lungs,
muscles stretched between each rib. And then,
pulling back of lips, and twisted tongue,
saying, "light and sky, torrential rain."

Another breath whistled through teeth reveals
mountains, the silver flash of turning leaves.
Desert sifts from sea, and all that breathe
atmosphere from those whom it would choke.

Exchanged from mouth to mouth, a final breath
gives voice to clay: first chatter, then a name—
too many names, for what already was:
things that fly, or swim, or give live birth.

But as the Holy Prankster found, when tickling
the diaphragm, so Adam quickly learned,
that words are metaphor for what is nothing
(or little) more than one's delight in breathing.

5

Beyond the curtain, building tops, the sky,
rather, just below that vantage point
a second sky was strung, refracting, no,
absorbing noonday sun in sheets of pink,

till telephones were silenced in their cradles
and we lost faith the mail would ever reach
lover, friend, or next-door neighbor, much less
convey communication from a god.

Despite the worst, a package did arrive,
neatly wrapped and metered, small enough
to slip into a purse or blazer pocket.
Forgotten. That is, till now, or times like now.

A prayer—awkward, difficult to hold—
fills my hands and mouth as words unfold.

6

Forgive that I was bred a princeling,
the well-fed laugh that comes from knowing,
no matter how I've misbehaved,
I'm loved, well-loved. Forgive the fact
I covet peace above all else,
ignore offence: unwelcome hand
along the thigh, the threat that follows.
And more, forgive that I've forgiven.

But if, my friend, finding your own
wounds still haven't healed, envy
renders mute the pardoning tongue.
Beware. For like the serpent, vexed,
writhing under spiteful tread,
I bite—piercing skin, tendon—crack
open bone, and poison marrow
with malice pressed from ripened wrath.

7

Whether crystalline spheres revolving one
inside the other, or a planetary
system held in measure by the Sun,
I am at creation's center, where I
live contented knowing the ordinary:
loved one, friend (and enemy, perhaps),
is all the world that I can hope to grasp.

8

I own this town: its people, and the zoo.
I own the bank, the barber shop, and diner,
and lease a bench to every truant minor,
or gangster with an octopus tattoo.

The mayor, city planners don't have a clue.
How could they? busy running trains on time,
sweeping tree-lined streets, and stopping crime.
No one can forestall my covert coup.

I take possession street by avenue;
catalogue each tenant, child, and pet,
who shares or sublets, who's amassed a debt
to buy a Brownstone with a River View.

I hold no deed, collect no revenue;
it's not the buildings, rather what they hold:
my town's the stories, songs, and lies I mold;
capital once tapped, profits accrue.

9

Shade drawn against the street lamp's flick,
refracting shades of silver, black,
as muscles shift along the back.
In corners shadows lurch like cats:
bedroom dance of acrobats.
This is love's arithmetic,
where nightly one and one are made
one silhouette against the shade.

10

Hair cropped short, close shaved, I tighten tie
around starched collar, lace black polished brogues
and clutch briefcase. This bird has learned to fly:
my first job . . . listen how my mother brags.

One home — computer, clock and Frigidaire —
dismantled, freighted uptown, reassembled,
to make a new one. Fed up with solitaire,
we play the pair, despite how much is gambled.

And you, not first, nor new, have set the pace,
my running mate, as life began or changed.
Your love's the detour off the karmic rat-race,
my destination no longer prearranged.

Fred Dings

Dido

When he left to plow the sea and husband
other lands, she became all fire.
The flames clutched air, their smoke

coiled over the city and frayed among
clouds and seaward wind. Her soul weighed
on the pyre, then plunged beneath embers,

thrusting into the dark like a root
to the waters of misery. She wandered
in wastelands and night, robed in the fire

of new arrivals. Others who had darkened
inside their cloaks withdrew from her
like ships among the trees. Her form glared

through the woods. Her stares scorched all
they tried to hold. The littering leaves
burned beneath her feet. She sought the nets

of branches, but none could hold her close enough.
She could not find a swamp to douse
herself in its pools or a river to drown

herself in its embrace. So she wandered,
a fire wrapped in fire. Once, *he* came,
pleading, armored, but she had considered

the nature of ships, the loading and unloading,
the angling of sails for wind, considered
the nature of harbors, open for whatever

sea-weary fates come sailing in.
Therefore her ears were closed when he spoke
as if from underwater on the sea's bed.

She choked the words before they could be born,
then clenched inside her fire and wrenched away.
But after that turning inward, she changed.

At first, desire dulling to despair, she started
to darken like the rest, but then no longer
wandered the woods: she stood among the trees

discerning the shades of shade, the way
loneliness shifted into solitude.
Her glances lingered with understanding,

which frightened many, and tremors of speech
broke the silence in that region.
She lightened as the heavy blood of self

drained from her fire, and saffron dawn
welled from a fissure in her breast, spreading
over her soul. She smiled, listening to those

who came to her, and consoled them as they took
her light. A glow lingered wherever
she walked. The fragrance of her compassion

incensed the dark. Faces emerged from cowls
and shone, reflecting her affection. So many
gathered, illumined, a pale and fallen heaven.

There was some question of further punishment.
The Light and the Dark were in dispute,
but in the end, Hell wanted her there

to feed the flames of the damned. Her kindness
would fester as their greatest points of pain,
the seeds of heaven they could never gain.

Heaven too required that she stay to show
all souls how miracles grow from misery
like roses growing from a bed of coals.

Bob Darling

Carolyn Cooke

Bob Darling spent the day and the evening on the fastest train in Europe. The train lugged slowly through yellow towns, then it began to pull together its force and go. The landscape slid past. In one stroke the train braced and broke through the air into a river of dinning sound. It climaxed at 380 km/h. Darling heard this news from a German across the aisle, but he sensed the speed in a deeper bone. His body was attuned to the subtle flux of high speed, to the jazz pulse, the fizz.

He closed his eyes, registered the scrape of the antimacassar against his brittle hairs, and dozed. Dying tired him, so did the drugs he took to keep from urinating on the seat. But he never let himself go that far, to close his eyes, unless the buzz of speed was in him, the drone of engines, the *zhzhzh* of jets.

On the seat beside him lounged a young woman named Carla. So far she had not given him too many terrible disappointments. Otherwise, she was a baby, vague on facts and ahistorical; she talked too much, she pouted when she didn't get her way, she disliked opera and she drank. But overall Darling felt they had been compatible. Paris, coming up, would be the last leg of their trip. Darling planned the Tuileries, the Orangerie, an afternoon at the Louvre, couscous in the Latin Quarter, two nights at the Hotel Angleterre.

That would be the end of it, then, no further obligation. Back home they would pass each other on the usual streets, exchange shrill pleasantries, pat each other's dogs. Sometime, perhaps, in the future, he could take her out to dinner at their old place on Bleecker Street and afterward press himself upon her as a lover. (With liquor enough, she had a sentimental heart.) But one day she would move, get a job, find a lover, change her life. She would look at her calendar and think she had not seen him on the street. But she would be afraid, so she would procrastinate about calling him until she was sure that he was dead. Then she would realize it must have happened a year, two years ago. And this way she would not mourn his passing.

(What would that be like? What if he didn't know, if the end of it was not-knowing, if not-knowing was the surprise? What if there was nothing afterward, and he didn't know? Where would the information go he had put into his head over the years—the names of kings, the taste of food, the memory of his mother and his father, that *Louvre* is early French for "leper," lava is mainly water, loose facts, what Thoreau said: "Our moulting season, like that of fowls, must be a crisis in our lives," the names of women, the names of small hotels? Would the contents of his busy head be wasted, lost?)

He opened his eyes. A crowd of old men on bicycles crashed by outside the window and were gone. Carla in the seat beside him leaned into the *Blue Guide*; the lemony point of her nose and the book vibrated perceptibly to the motion of the train. Her eyes were puffy, from sleep maybe. She still had on her dress from the evening before—it was an absurd dress for day—and some cosmetic residue sparkled on her throat. Her sharp perfume hung on the air. She could sit for hours that way, a packet of French cigarettes and a bottle of Perrier balanced on the seat beside her, her bare feet crossed in her lap. She read any trash for hours and ignored the view. Travel, Darling thought irritably, was a vacation for her.

"The *Train à Grande Vitesse*," she said now, out of nowhere.

"The TGV, yes, that's the train we're on now," he said.

"You called it the *Très Grande Vitesse*," said Carla, looking up at him, frowning. "Actually it's *train*, not *très*."

"That's what they call it informally, I guess," he said, looking across Carla's lap at the blur of France. "Very Great Speed."

"Informally they call it the TGV. And I know what *très* means, thank you."

She was a little bulldog, round face, skinny as a refugee, knees like knuckles in stripey tights. Long arms, down to her knees. Twenty, twenty-two. He was not an old man, Darling, but compared to her. But in her eyes. From that first afternoon he thought he could get her into bed if he remembered to call her Carla, not Paula.

He had found her in a funny way, unconscious on another train. There were two of them almost exactly alike. It was a hot summer day; they looked as if they had been to the beach. Sun sparkled on the backs of their necks and the strings of their bathing suits dangled down, one red checked, the other pale blue. The strings held up the brassieres of their suits, the only word for it he knew.

They hung from the handstraps, limp as fringe. First one girl went down. The shoes of interested citizens chattered like sets of teeth around the head. Then the second girl dropped straight as a rope. The shoes, aroused by one girl unconscious, lost interest. Two girls down stank of conspiracy. No one besides Bob Darling wanted to be taken in.

He hiked his trousers so they would not be damaged by his knees and squatted to greet the girls when they woke. In the dangerous and unpredictable city, maybe this gesture had saved their lives. He ought to be able to get one of them into bed.

The first one opened her eyes, and he saw a flattening out of the tube of her pupils, her vision narrowing to familiar and unimaginative suspicions. "What did I, pass out?" she said.

"You seemed to fall," Darling said.

The girl blinked at him. "My wallet still here?" she slapped her body with her hands, then quieted them in a leather pouch around her belly. "Miracle."

"You want air," he said.

She shook her head. "I've got to go to work downtown." It was a shame, Darling thought, because the first girl really was the up-and-comer.

"What do you do? I mean that respectfully," Darling assured her, because he thought she might be a dancer, and Paula had been the most marvellously uninhibited dancer. His response to her dancing had always been sexual, but in the most respectful sense.

"Legal proofreading," said the girl.

The second girl opened her eyes and he looked away from the first girl into her face. She was a bulldog, but not bad looking.

The first girl changed trains to downtown. Darling marvelled at how they bussed each other's cheeks, then one went off to read legal documents in an office, sand still sparkling on the back of her neck. That pale blue string.

He walked the second girl—Carla—up from the underground. He held her arm. He liked to think he knew the why and the how of the city. Did she know the such and such café? The apple cake was the thing to eat. Did she like apple cake? He guided her into the café's perimeter by the arm.

But Carla didn't want apple cake. She said she was bored without drinks. She sat across a round table, behind a tumbler of yellow wine.

He was old enough that she would not be shocked by the news of his death, or the idea of his illness. "Things break down," she would think with a shrug. But Darling was still young enough—and the news was fresh enough—that it came as a shock, a surprise. Barely two hours before he found her, his GP, Carnevali, had sighed deeply and told Darling to

Concentrate
on the probability
of mortality.

Darling had buttoned down his shirt, top to bottom. He covered up his lung, his large intestine, his small intestine, his appendicitis scar. He put on his sweater and his leather jacket. He was about to hail a taxi on Park when suddenly he wanted to live, live. His eyes flailed like arms, grasping at the colors of the city. He had crossed over to Lexington, and grabbed the subway downtown.

His apple cake lay in crumbs before him on a plate. "Let me show you something," he said, throwing out a spark of spit. He removed a black leather book and a fountain pen from inside his jacket pocket. A lozenge flew out too and rolled wildly into the gutter. He leaned over the book, showing it to her, partially blocking her view with his body, intent. "This is Dwight Sterling," he said, and pointed to a list of numbers. "First-rate accountant." He looked at Carla. "You don't do your own taxes, do you? This is his office, this is home—his wife's name is Paula, you'll like her, she is very uninhibited. This is their number in Springs. Dwight can get a message to me anytime. Now here is Jane, she is the astrologer who walks my dog—you can call her. This is Herb Witter, he's a philosopher. He left academia to sell industrial properties in Elizabeth, New Jersey. These are people who can get a message to me anytime," he said.

He closed the book and slid it across the table. "You take it. I know all these numbers." Her hand flickered on the table. "Please," he said. "Even if you don't *want* to leave a message I will know you *can* leave a message."

"See your pen?" she said. He handed it over. She opened his little address book to a blank page near the *W*s and rolled the pen across it experimentally. Then she drew an outline of the couple at the next table, and the table, and a vase with a few flowers in it.

Darling jiggled his leg. "You're an artist," he said.

"Naah." She ran blue lines through her drawings. He watched her bear down on the nib. He smiled, sipped his coffee. "That's a hundred-and-fifty-dollar pen," he said.

Her face emptied. She slipped the cap on the pen and slid it across the table.

"No, no, you use it," he said.

Her finger touched the marbled end.

Darling scraped his chair on the concrete, hobbled it over in a series of shrieks and told her his name. "You can call me Bob, or you can call me Darling. I mean that respectfully. Most people call me Darling. Not just women. Men."

"Darling," she said. "Like the girl in Peter Pan."

"What? Peter Pan?" Darling said excitedly.

"The girl's name—the one who goes to Never-land with Peter Pan."

"Not Mary Martin?"

"No—I meant—the Disney," she said.

Darling sniffed. "Life is too short to talk about Walter Disney," he said.

"Fine," she said. She looked at the pen.

It was their first frisson. Darling savored it with coffee. Together they watched the couple she had drawn eat a big meal at the next table, two halves of chicken—but possibly not the same chicken. They sat across from each other, looking at their dinners. The man ate delicately, pulling the underdone meat away from the bone with the point of his knife and actually penetrating his mouth with the blade. He fixed his yellow eyes impersonally on the food. The woman ate quickly, as if other duties called to her. His thin white shirt strained to girdle him, and through the fabric the white loops of his undershirt were legible. The woman wore a transparent blouse which magnified her white arms and the vastness of her brassiere. Once she stopped chewing, looked up at him and said something. The man didn't look at her, but barked out a laugh. "I'm not feeling flush tonight," he said.

They ate the skin off their chicken, buttered their bread and rolled it up so more fit into their mouths in one bite. When all the food was gone they wiped their lips with their napkins and waited with all their attention until the waiter came and cleared their plates away.

When the waiter came back with pie and coffee on a tray

their hands flew up to make room for the dishes, fingers like birds' wings. They took turns using the cream and sugar. The woman stirred her coffee. "Everything I've dreamed of for forty years, its coming true," she said loudly.

Darling squeezed Carla's hand. "Are you hungry?" he asked.

"Oh, no. I never eat at night," she said.

He climbed six flights of stairs to her one room of Chinese paper lanterns and museum posters and her futon on the floor battened down with sheets and a quilt and ropes of lingerie and clothes. They sat on the futon, which was all of her furniture. There was an old coal fireplace with a flue out one side, but the blue rug ran into it. She served him a glass of yellow wine. Everything she had, she offered.

She played Stravinsky's *Firebird* on her boom box and rolled pink lipstick over her lips. When she stood and rolled her thin sweater up her arms and called him to her bed, he realized he was already there. The slug of strong sensations—desire, hope, *virility*—brought tears of sorrow to his eyes, which Carla mistook for gratitude.

He hoped to keep his bag of sensations light. Only the most intense sensations interested him. He had looked forward to this train because it was the fastest train. He had been very clear with Carla about this from the start. He wanted to ride the fastest train in Europe. That was one. Two was, he wanted to eat the wonderful six-course dinner they served on the train. If they went together, this was something he definitely wanted to do. He asked her all about it before they left the city, while they were still in the planning stages.

"Fine Bob, whatever," Carla said when he asked.

Some afternoons they sat under a sun umbrella at the such and such café. Her accent, when she ordered *caffè macchiato*, was perfect. Darling spread out the map like a tablecloth under their cups and crumbs and napkins and brought out sheets of onionskin scribbled over in pencil with the itinerary, flight numbers, trian routes and the names and telephone numbers and addresses of hotels. He noticed that Carla used these things carefully. She brushed his cake crumbs from the countries on the map.

She had never heard of Versailles, Père-Lachaise. She had never heard of Jim Morrison. Her ignorance was vast, ecumenical. He drew on the paper cloth with a mechanical pencil—he had given over his fountain pen and hadn't seen it since. He sketched dreamily, from memory.

"What's that?" she asked.

"It's a baguette, a kind of long French bread."

"Oh, Bob, I know *baguette*. I thought you were drawing a canoe."

But then he thought she spoke Italian from her seamless demand for *macchiato*. She shrugged and said she didn't know a word of it—just liked the bitterness. He wondered whether she had broken his pen, bearing down on the nib, or sold it. He would have liked to show her how the ink went in so that if the pen had stopped working she would not worry that she was to blame. His heart ached, imagining her humiliation and shy gratitude.

"You have to speak up—it won't be any good unless we do things you want to do," he told her. "We have to plan everything together. You have to tell me where you want to go, what you want to see."

Carla had never been there before. "I don't know," she said. Her white dress was ancient unto transparency. Her shoulders looked like two milk bottles.

He had read that the dinners on the train were sometimes oversubscribed. You could eat a *croque monsieur* in the bar car, but that wasn't the thing to do. The thing to do was to get the dinner on the train.

"Fine, whatever," Carla said. "I don't care what I eat."

He leaned across the table, angry, closed his fingers around Carla's wrist, and squeezed.

She pulled his hand off in a smooth strong gesture which

surprised him and pulled her arm into her lap. "I eat anything. Scraps," she said.

He sat up late at night on the floor walled in by forty years' worth of *The New York Times* and creased hotel brochures. He called her at two o'clock in the morning. "Do you want to go to the Sabine Hills or the Villa d'Este at Tivoli? Tell me what you want to do."

There was a pause on the line, a certain flattening out in the expectant air. "Who is this, please?" she said.

And yet, in Europe, it turned out Carla had a terrible instinct for knowing exactly what she wanted to do. In Venice she saw the Lido from a speedboat and wanted to go there. "What is it?" she said, and he told her.

"Oh, Bob, I want to go and spend a day," she said.

But she had agreed already, he reminded her, buttoning his shirt, to walk with him through the *Collezione Peggy Guggenheim*, and to take a vaporetto to the cathedral at Torcello. Anyway, the last time he had been to the Lido the water was full of white fuzz balls and nobody would swim.

"But I want to go to the Lido," she objected. "Just rent a beach chair if it isn't too expensive. I just want to be there, Bob." She jumped up and down on the bed, then jumped off and ran to the window and pulled back the heavy curtain.

"I doubt you can even get your lunch out there," he said. "I thought we could sit at a table in the Piazza San Marco."

"Oh, Bob, I don't want to eat!" Carla said. "I could just go out on the boat taxi and meet you later."

They stood barefoot on the rug, facing each other across the unmade bed.

"If that's what you would like to do," he said.

"It is, it is," she said.

And it was done.

He spent the day on foot, a blind day of moving through the crowds at the Piazza San Marco, leaning on the arm of the vaporetto, sliding through the viscous water to the mud-

flats, on foot again across the Bridge of Sighs. Always water
swelled under him, undulating, filthy blackness. He smelled
his own sweat through the leather jacket and tasted in his
mouth the temperature of his boiling insides. After lunch in
a trattoria in Dorsoduro he went out in the air and coughed
two drops of blood on a Kleenex. He folded the Kleenex into
the pocket of his leather jacket and went on to the piazza,
where he threw the Kleenex away.

Hours later he opened the door to his room with his key.
The ether of wine was like a fog, an oriental smokiness. Carla
was sitting straddled across the bidet with just the top of the
bikini on that she had bought in a newsstand at the beginning
of their trip, before they left the U.S., even. Even then he
had been shocked by that crudeness, that lack of care. He
remembered paying a hotel bill, while she went off into the
newsstand, sliding a card from his wallet, signing his name.
That unpleasantness, a woman beside him with a bag in one
hand and a bottle of mouthwash in the other, having some
trouble about her bill, putting the bottle of mouthwash down
on the cashier's polished desk, and raking a hand through her
bag, her hair ugly around the neck of her coat, muttering
"*Merde, merde* . . . "

Carla's skin was burnt red around the bathing suit top and
she had long scratch marks up and down her back. She turned
slowly away from the sound of running water to look at him
in the door. Twisting her chin over her shoulder pulled cords
in her throat which opened her mouth. She seemed to be
manipulated by strings.

Some bleary look in her eyes got in the way of his concern
for her.

He folded his leather jacket over his arm. He stood in the
doorway with the door in one hand. "I may just meet you
downstairs," he said.

Carla rolled her eyes and turned away. He went out, closing
the door behind him. He bought a postcard at the front desk
and sat down at a narrow writing desk.

"Dear Paula," he wrote. "It is now six o'clock Sunday evening. The clock atop the Italian steps has struck those hours

with an ancient quality. An array of birds with a multiplicity of sounds is announcing their departure this evening. The light is muted and pink, the city overall is waiting." He read it over—it all seemed beside the point somehow. She had been so direct with him in her postcard from Helsinki, the small block letters: "You are an elf, darling. But I am not really interested in elves."

He folded the card over and over itself and slipped it into his pocket just as Carla appeared in the doorway. She had on her small black thrift-store dress; she had pushed her yellow hair back behind tiny pearls in her ears. But under her eyes looked yellow-blue. They had Pellegrino water together, then dinner at a place on one of the canals, pasta first, then calamari in ink and, at Darling's suggestion, three bottles of wine. "How many bottles do we need?" Darling asked Carla. "I mean that respectfully. I want to get drunk too." They drank fast out of tiny green glasses. Bob Darling shouted, "I'm drunk! Pow! Life is a glorious mist!"

He ordered cake and a gondola, and then the ancient wooden walls began to close in around him. His vision closed down on her dress, which seemed to have no front or back. Someone had laid a round plate of cake on her chest (between her breasts, nipples like eyes), which one of the waiters passed to the gondolier on the boat after he passed Carla, who was laughing, out.

She held his arm on the ride back to the hotel. Looking out over the black water he pictured the way he would open the world to her, the blown-glass choker he would fit around her neck, the lire liquid in his hand, pouring into her. His fingers spread around the knuckle of her knee.

"You want to know what my landlady said about you, Bob?"

"If you like," he said.

"It was the time you told that terrible joke, remember? She said, 'I don't trust one single thing about that man.' " She squeezed his arm.

On the way out of the gondola she slipped and her leg sank into the black liquid up to her knee. Walking up the narrow stairs to their room he heard the sucking sound of her shoe.

Then she was asleep, painful-looking, red. He tried not to look at her, at the red marks on her back. Instead he lay back on his pillow, unable as ever to sleep in silence, and turned pages in the blank book he had bought for her to record her trip. "He was his own whole world," she had written. "He wore neat black suits, bikini underwear. Every day he sent his pajamas down to be washed — why? — and they came back ironed. He saved anything that had words on it — theater tickets, programs, newspapers, napkins — but he never read anything. He carried a skin change purse that I wanted. He could walk for hours without stopping, but only in the city. He gave out his telephone numbers to everyone."

Her hand flopped out and lay on his arm. He looked at her things from the day tossed out like ropes at sea — her bikini bottom, the black dress, the plate and fork and the remains of the cake they had eaten on the boat, the Oriental smell of her perfume, the ether of wine. He read more, snatches here and there — her block letters were full of effort but difficult to read. "Asked if he could cut me just a little bit on the thigh with his nail scissors." (His eye shot up, electric, red, but fell again to the page.) "In an umber room/ he kissed my mouth/ nibbled my mouth like an ant/ carried me away/ like crumbs." He let Carla's hand lie on his arm until it felt heavy, then he moved it away.

The argument was about the difference between naked and nude. They had it in France, in the countryside, over dinner in a small hotel. His cutlet had a crust on it and it swam in a sauce. He drank wine from a leaden pitcher.

"My friend Paula one time gave a dinner party," he said, mentioning Paula carefully, by name. "All her husband's clients, all their Oriental rugs unrolled, and she just came into the room and unzipped this jumpsuit she was wearing and it just fell around her feet like a puddle. I'll never forget it. She was naked, she was statuesque, celebrating, inviting, brave. To say she was nude is an insult."

"What did people do?" Carla asked.

"Of course no one did anything. We were far too respectful.

A woman like Paula naked in a room like that is almost untouchable."

"But what was it for?" Carla asked.

"You mean, did she want to be an object of art or an object of sex? Isn't that what you mean, you think these things are different?"

Carla said, "Poor Paula."

"Why?" He could hear the mockery in his voice. Spit formed in the corner of his mouth. Was it finer to be painted by Picasso than to stand naked at a window? Which picture would be finer, better?

But the word he used was wrong, she argued. You would never say a child was nude — it would be an offense to the child, it would be obscene. Nudity corrupted nakedness with eyes, she said, climbing up onto her high horse, conservative as a child.

Would she prefer the lighter and more moral state? he asked her, mocking. Which was the more "natural" state? If nudity was more artful than nakedness, wasn't it also less natural? So it followed, since she was always interested in being more natural, that she would rather get naked than get nude.

"I am not interested in being more natural," she said.

He sent his dinner back twice. It was an impossible place. He went upstairs to the loo; through a hole in the floor he saw the top of her head, saw her spear a corner of his cutlet with her fork. Flies, flies. Standing over the urinal, he understood he was dying of foie gras and sauternes. Their room down the hall — she had flung the casement open and let in all the flies. But what could it matter? He buttoned up his pants and hell, hell, did not wash his hands.

After dinner she wanted to go for a walk — through the fields of sunflowers.

"All right," he said. He wanted to hurt her so she would remember him. But it was hard to walk without seeing his feet, through the wide yellow heads bobbing in his. His hand attached to her damp shoulder with a sound of suction.

"Your eyes are so Freud," she said.

"What did you say?"

"Freud, in German it means cold."

He took hold of the other shoulder.

"Do you think you tricked me? Do you think you're crafty?" she burst out. She pushed him off, away. He fell back, pulling the heavy-headed flowers down with him. He pulled at her arm with his hand, pulling her to him, calling her to bring him up. He felt the wide universe between him and the world. She yanked wildly at his arm and there was the door of the pensione, the closed white stone.

The train reeled north at great speed. Carla opened her eyes, stretched her arms and yawned. She looked out of the window. "What time is it?" she asked.

"Five o'clock," he said. "We have dinner in half an hour."

She sat up now, serious, and rolled orange lipstick over her lips, examining her mouth in a pocket mirror inscribed, she had told him, to her mother by a lover: "A little bit every day." She closed the mirror and dropped it into one of her shapeless bags. "Oh, I can't eat at 5:30, can you Bob? Let's go and have a drink in the bar."

It was unbelievable. He could have pulled out her eyes.

"I asked you a month ago about eating dinner on this train," he said.

"Don't you see what this is? All they are going to do is throw a tray at you," she said.

The train overtook its whistle. All sound now was behind his ears. He had an image of himself in black space, pinned on the back of a rocket. He put his arms down like two great weights on the armrests—to steady himself.

"Please, eat this dinner with me," he said.

"Look," said Carla, "Why can't we just go into the bar car and have a drink and a sandwich or something later, when we get hungry? I can't stand being crammed in this car like a sardine. Wouldn't it be more interesting to go and have a drink and look out the windows and talk to people?"

"I don't want to," Darling said. "What I want to do is what we arranged a month ago. I want to eat the dinner they serve on this train. I want to sit right here and eat the dinner they serve on the train!"

"Oh, I don't," she said.

"You wanted to a month ago when you said you would," he said.

"Oh, Bob, for God's sake, a month ago." She raked her hair with a hand and looked over the tops of the seats at the people sitting in seats all around them, at the oblivious heads.

"Eat dinner with me tonight. Please, Carla, just do it," he said.

"Why do you want me to do something I don't want to do? Why would you want that?" she said. Her eyes went everywhere but to him.

He looked at Carla until she ran out of places to look, until she couldn't go anywhere, until she looked at him. He sat in her path, in the aisle seat. Carla had the window. Her eyes floated over him.

"I don't see the point of asking me to sit here and eat my dinner on a tray when I am not hungry and I don't want to do it."

"Could you do something for me just because I ask you to, or do you think dinner is too much to ask? Because it wasn't too much to ask a month ago when I asked you. According to you it wasn't," he said. He looked at his fingers vibrating in his lap, melded into a warped hideous undifferentiated hand, a paw.

Her eyes glazed over. She looked past him.

He hugged his knees to his seat's edge and let her climb over him into the aisle. She stood up and stretched herself out limb by limb like an animal. He looked up, and she rolled her green eyes over him.

"I need francs," she said.

He reached into his shirt and pulled out the skin purse she had coveted. "Take it," he said.

She caressed the skin between her fingers, tears in her eyes. "Look, Bob, I'm sorry I've been this big disappointment to you on your trip," she said. "I did my best, okay?"

He looked into her face for any sign but there was none.

"Okay, Bob?" Carla said again.

"Take the River Styx to hell!" he said.

She walked backward toward the bar car, against the speed and pull of the train. Her fingers moved over the skin purse; it was the scrotum of a lamb. A steward brought two trays— chicken breasts in white sauce, yellow beans, apple tarts.

He sat quietly, penned into his seat by his tray. He looked across the seat Carla had left and at the tray on the folding table in front of it, and beyond that out of the window at the blur of France. He considered moving into her seat, but then considered the empty seat to be part of his view: not-Carla. He tasted his unpromising dinner and discovered that he was hungry, but still discerning.

He ate his dinner slowly, looking carefully across the empty seat at the blur, and at Carla's chicken, at her yellow bones. All right: it was the fastest train in Europe. The food was above average. Everything was moving. The landscape outside looked as if it were underwater, wet, bleeding green-yellow-blue. He gripped a tray in each hand and in one motion switched his empty tray with hers. He ate the second dinner more quickly than the first, kept the fork gripped in his hand and moving back and forth between the tray and his mouth until he had to confess he was glad she had left. He scooped up Carla's apple tart, then wiped the ooze from his lips with a napkin, virtuous. He looked at the outside from the inside of the train. There was no comparison between this train and other trains he had ridden. He was like a fish being carried upriver in a current faster than a fish could swim. In the cradle of this unanswerable motion, Bob Darling rested and slept. The river poured into his eyes.

Letters

The letters that follow are in response to Harold Bloom's assertion (in his interview — issue 136 — in which he offered a canon of Western humor) that the only woman author worthy of being called a humorist is Jane Austen.

Dear Constant Reader Bloom,

I find your humor canon impressive yet, to quote Dorothy Parker, the breadth of your choices remains "a rhinestone in the rough." I can scarcely believe that throughout your interview on the canon of western humor Jane Austen was the only woman writer you identified as being truly funny. Indeed, this reader must confess that she has never found Austen particularly amusing and has never, going by your standard of determining what is humorous, laughed out loud while reading one of her novels. But then you admit in your interview that humor is extremely difficult to define. Not that I would for a moment discount that Austen genuinely strikes your funny bone; however, I find myself in good company in my dissension. Mark Twain, whom you greatly admire for his vernacular humor, as do I, hated Austen. In fact during the last fifteen years of his life Twain's contempt for Austen was so great that merely the mention of her name would send him into apoplectic fits. Twain's comment on *Pride and Preju-*

dice, the work you find so entertaining, was that every time he read it he was tempted to "dig her up and beat her over the skull with her own shin-bone." Since I find Twain a "genu-wyne" funny man, I thought it might be of interest to mention here just a few of the women Twain did find humorous with whom you may not be familiar. The first is Marietta Holley, who published poetry as well as contributed to the American vernacular-humor tradition in her twenty-plus novels, among them *My Opinions and Betsey Bobbet's* and *Samantha at Saratoga*. During the 1880s and 1890s Holley was such a celebrated humorist that her popularity rivaled Twain's. Twain, inarguably a good judge of wit, included Holley on his list of humorists to be published by the American Publishing Company in the anthology *Mark Twain's Library of Humor* — Twain's own bit of canonizing. Another writer Twain admired and published was Mary Mapes Dodge. Her short story "Miss Malony on the Chinese Question" was included in *Twain's Library of Humor*. Dodge also wrote a satirical response to a poem by Jenny Parker decrying an untrue love that was published. The last stanza of Dodge's response follows:

> Take this advice and get him back,
>   My darling, if you can,
> And if you can't, why — right about,
>   And take another man!

Last to be mentioned here, but by no means least, is the writer and lecturer Anna Dickinson. Now just a forgotten footnote for literary historians, in her day Dickinson was a nationally important figure. Her clout was such that Lincoln had to ask her twice before she agreed to support his re-election campaign. Twain admired Dickinson's oratorical skill and was jealous of her ability to outearn him on the lecture circuit. Dickinson's specialty was her biting delivery; in one lecture she commented, "There may be a great many women not married today who will be married some time in the future, and to some of those present I shall in advance tender my most hearty and sincere commiseration. There are women who will not be married at all, and to some of these I will tender my congratulations." This was quite acerbic material for 1867.

Does it matter that these women mentioned above would be unknown to Constant Reader? Not particularly, as Twain says, "whenever I take up *Pride and Prejudice* I feel like a barkeeper entering the Kingdom of Heaven." In saying this Twain meant that after repeatedly trying to recognize the "high art" in Austen's novel acclaimed by respected critics he was ultimately left to trust his own taste. And following Twain's cue, so shall I. Clearly, while providing a detailed history of one gender Constant Reader does manage some rather startling omissions. As for his observation that women seem to lack a sense of humor because they are in contention with the whole world of male writers, why I can only surmise that Constant Reader is either making a wee witticism or has his head in a *sac en papier* and cannot see the joke for the gender. Why it can be just as easily argued that the reason particular women writers and poets possess such a well-developed sense of humor is *because* they must deal with the world of male writers — should one take all of Norman Mailer's prose seriously?

Now it is tempting to start listing women who employ humor in their writing (Fanny Fern, Frances Whitcher, Virginia Woolf), yet such cataloging would simply create yet another personalized list (Erica Jong, Anne Sexton, Maya Angelou) and I will try and resist such seductive canonizing (Gertrude Stein, Grace Paley, Elaine May). Instead I will restrict myself to a few comments in reaction to Constant Reader's pronouncements. While Constant Reader most distinctly does not find Edith Wharton funny, at times I do. Her short story "Roman Fever" is a triumph of female cattiness masquerading as feminine docility. As one reads through the layers of the story and reaches the sublime last line, "I had Barbara," this can only be read with a snort and shriek — or you didn't get the joke. I appreciate Constant Reader's enthusiasm for W.C. Fields and the Mack Sennett comedies, though it baffles me that Mae West doesn't rate a mention. After all, West and Fields

costarred and West cowrote "My Little Chickadee" with Fields.
If I had to choose comics I'd pick a dimpled Mae West over
a flaccid W.C. Fields any day. Finally our divergent tastes in
humor do meet in your selection of Oscar Wilde. I agree entirely. Wilde is a riot (when I was a child my cousins and I
would label anyone capable of rendering us incoherent with
laughter "a riot" — Moms Mabley, Carol Burnett, Lily Tomlin).
I have always found Wilde hilarious in a pointed, nasty kind of
way. Only one other writer matches Wilde's sublime bitchiness
and that would be Dorothy Parker, an Algonquin regular,
who had this to say about Wilde:

> If, with the literate, I am
> Impelled to try an epigram,
> I never seek to take the credit;
> We all assume that Oscar said it.

But not always, Constant Reader; let's give the funny
women their credit.

Laura Skandera-Trombley
Associate Professor
State University of New York at Potsdam

Dear Editor,

It is lamentable that in Harold Bloom's off-the-cuff attempt
to define a "Canon of Western Humor" (*The Paris Review*
#136), he is unable to think of any major women comic writers,
with the notable exception of Jane Austen. More unfortunate
still is his assumption that because he cannot think of any,
they do not exist.

Bloom's inability to come up with women writers to add
to his canon of humor (in spite of George Plimpton's efforts to
get him to do so) points to larger problems in canon-formation,
and specifically, in canonizing humorous texts. As Bloom him-

self admits, "definitions of humor have never worked," or as the great lexicographer Samuel Johnson put it when he attempted to define comedy in an installment of *The Rambler*, "definitions are hazardous." So much depends upon where one stands in relation to the humor, a point that Bloom implies when he says that "it's a question of perspectivism." Bloom's own touchstones of humor—for instance, the "epigraph" he provides from Oscar Wilde—would certainly not elicit universal laughter. In fact, the whole notion of a joke or humorous piece that would be universally funny is impossible to envision, given the wide variety of customs, mores, values and so forth that are contained within this planet as universe.

One might argue that "Western" narrows things down a bit, but it really only serves to obfuscate the central fact that canons are based upon assumptions that everyone in the West might not hold. Russians and Germans would, I am sure, take offense at Bloom's disregard for their nations' humor. However, in dismissing the humor of women, Bloom makes a cross-cultural assertion that is not only unwarranted, but stands within a fairly long and insidious tradition of viewing women as utterly humorless. Without claiming that the sense of humor in men and women is fundamentally different, I would like to assert that women's humor has been overlooked in canons of humor because of the perspectives of those who have decided what counts as humor.

"Here today, gone tomorrow" might serve as the epigraph for women's humorous writing, and it is appropriate that the witty and entertaining Restoration playwright Aphra Behn has been credited with the first usage of this phrase. Despite ample evidence of its existence, women's humor has until recently remained something of a well-kept secret. Even when women are acknowledged as humorous writers in their day, their works have typically dropped out of the canon because of the content of the humor, especially in cases where patriarchy is the butt of their jokes (a fruitful topic for humor and satire, as one might imagine). For political reasons, women have had to exercise caution in sharing their jokes. A woman who laughs at "the man" might find herself out on the street. The kitchen—

women's exclusive domain — was often the only safe place for laughter. When women's humor does emerge beyond the kitchen doors and into the realm of print culture, it is often masked or encoded so that it can pass as acceptable in that male-controlled field.

Because of the circumscribed nature of women's comic practices, the notion that women have no sense of humor has been hard to dispel. Since humor often takes advantage of people's insecurities, it is no wonder that patriarchal males would try to keep women in their place by denying them a sense of humor. At the same time, many men have empowered themselves by asserting the quality of their own wit and demanding that women acknowledge their mastery. Women might laugh together behind closed doors, but their sense of humor has usually been measured according to how well they laugh in public at men's jokes.

Anthologies of men's wit and humor have offered examples of the kind of stuff women were supposed to grin and bear. In these collections, women frequently appear as the butts of male jokes. One twentieth-century reference book on humor, *Esar's Comic Dictionary* (1943), includes under the entry on "women" the following note: "This word has not been cross-referenced because it occurs very often in this dictionary." And indeed it does. From *A* ("assault . . . Every woman likes to be taken with a grain of assault") to *Z* ("zeal . . . A woman cherishes the memory of her first love-affair with the same zeal with which a man forgets his"), Esar makes it clear why women weren't laughing very hard.

Eighteenth- and nineteenth-century conceptions of female character are largely responsible for creating the myth of women's humorlessness in England and America. Virginia Woolf's witty characterization of the Angel in the House describes the feminine ideal quite aptly: "She was intensely sympathetic. She was immensely charming. She was utterly unselfish. She excelled in the difficult arts of family life. She sacrificed herself daily. If there was a chicken, she took the leg; if there was a draught, she sat in it — in short she was so constituted that she never had a mind or a wish of her own, but preferred to sympathize always with the minds and wishes of others. Above all — I need not say it — she was pure. Her purity was supposed to be her chief beauty — her blushes, her great grace." This feminine ideal (debunked successfully by Woolf's sketch) excised, along with sexuality, a sense of humor from female nature so effectively that by the end of the nineteenth century a common refrain held that women have no sense of humor at all. Thus, a writer for the *Saturday Review* begins his article on "Feminine Humour" (1871) with a received witticism: "The humour of women, it is said, resembles the snakes in Iceland. In other words it does not exist." This writer refers to ideal femininity in order to account for women's alleged humorlessness: "Women are too good to be humorists."

The idea that women have no sense of humor is one that a writer like Aphra Behn would not have had to combat. Playwrights such as Behn, Mary Pix and Susanna Centlivre found an audience for their comic talents in late seventeenth-century England. And in the eighteenth century, that great age of comedy, women novelists were flexing their comic muscles right along with the men. Charlotte Lennox's *Female Quixote*, with its outrageously funny send-up of contemporary ideas about women and courtship, deserves a place next to *Tom Jones* and *Tristram Shandy* among the great eighteenth-century comic novels. Her Arabella, an avid romance reader who — like her Spanish predecessor takes the stories as literal truth — is both comical and sympathetic, and Lennox's statement on satire still holds true: "When Actions are a Censure upon themselves, the Reciter will always be consider'd as a Satirist." Frances Burney's comic talents were highly regarded in her day and were almost certainly an inspiration to Charles Dickens; her Mr. Giles Arbe in *The Wanderer* is a near cousin of Dickens's Mr. Dick. All of Burney's novels are enlivened by humor and satire that stands up to the test of time. When Harold Bloom states, "It would be interesting if one could understand why it was that Miss Austen was able to be so piercingly funny," he might do well to consider that she cut her novelistic teeth on writers like Lennox, Burney and Maria Edgeworth (of *Castle Rackrent* fame).

Collections of women's humor—striving to implement a female canon of humor—fight against the prejudices of historians. Male authorities on comedy might valorize Mark Twain and forget that Marietta Holley rivaled him in public favor, but women's anthologies tell the other side of the story. Given the cultural injunction against female humor and the widespread disbelief in its existence, the task of researching the subject required dedication and zeal. It should come as no surprise, then, that the earliest collectors of women's humor tended to see themselves as missionaries out to convert a faithless audience. Two examples will serve to illustrate the work that such anthologies can do.

Kate Sanborn, who put together the very first women's humor collection in 1885, was inspired to undertake the task because of one man's printed assertion that humor "is the rarest of qualities in woman." As proof of women's comic talents, *The Wit of Women* ranges from the late seventeenth century to her own time. Sanborn concludes her collection with a witty epigram of her own, a challenge to any who might now dare to deny her evidence:

If you pronounce this book not funny,
And wish you hadn't spent your money.
There soon will be a general rumor
That you're no judge of Wit or Humor.

By refusing to bow down to male standards, Sanborn encourages her female readers to value women's jokes even when men say they're not funny. She indicates that women in a sexist society can assert their independence by laughing together.

Martha Bensley Bruère and Mary Ritter Beard in the 1934 anthology *Laughing Their Way* pay tribute to Sanborn's efforts and marvel at the change that seems to have taken place since their predecessor's work. In their day, they claim, "No one today can pick up a newspaper, read a magazine, or work in a library without meeting face to face laughing women who peer through the printed pages." Bruère and Beard assembled a gallery of laughing women whose names may be unfamiliar to the late twentieth-century reader, but whose works continue to speak incisively to present-day circumstances. For example, the suffragette columnist Alice Duer Miller attacks patriarchal hypocrisy with a satirical angle that is both part of its period and relevant beyond it:

> The New York State Association Opposed to Woman Suffrage is sending out leaflets to its members urging them to "tell every man you meet, your tailor, your postman, your grocer, as well as your *dinner partner*, that you are opposed to woman suffrage."
>
> We hope that the 90,000 sewing machine operatives, the 40,000 saleswomen, the 32,000 laundry operatives, the 20,000 knitting and silk mill girls, the 17,000 women janitors and cleaners, the 12,000 cigar-makers, to say nothing of the 700,000 other women and girls in industry in New York State, will remember when they have drawn off their long gloves and tasted their oysters to tell their dinner partners that they are opposed to woman suffrage because they fear it might take women out of the home.

Like so many other early books that celebrate women's accomplishments, Bruère and Beard's collection makes us recognize how standard canons have typically overlooked women's works. Nineteenth-century writers like Marietta Holley (Samantha Allen), Frances Barry Whitcher (The Widow Bedott), and Sara Willis Parton (Fanny Fern) — once widely recognized comic talents — are now known only to a handful of dedicated readers.

Even women writers who have been included in the canon of Western literature — Charlotte Brontë, George Eliot, Virginia Woolf — don't receive credit for their well-developed senses of humor, irony and satire. If Bloom finds *Jane Eyre* to be an angry work, he might consider its satirical thrust and think about a figure like Mr. Brocklehurst, whose message of "consistency" is completely — and comically — undercut by his blatant hypocrisy. Eliot's Mrs. Cadwallader and the bumbling Mr. Brooke are delightfully comic, and Mary Garth's witty tongue gives the lie to Bloom's claim that "there isn't a touch" of humor in Eliot. As for Woolf, *Orlando* is a rare example of a modernist comic novel, and even in a serious work, such as *A Room of One's Own*, wit and humor shine out on almost every page. To be sure, Woolf's humor walks a fine line between the tragic and the comic; however, to ignore her comic vision is to miss out on the human struggles that her works reflect.

To any examples I might offer, a critic might counter, "But that's not funny." I would respond to this critic with the words of the maligned George Eliot: "A difference of taste in jokes is a great strain on the affections." I am willing to concede that Bloom's "Canon of Western Humor" shoots straight in many cases, but his assessment of women writers is way off the mark, and I suggest that he widen his scope to include female comic talents. In addition to the writers I've mentioned, I would highly recommend as sources of British and American humor Lady Mary Wortley Montagu, Elizabeth Gaskell, Emily Dickinson, Dorothy Parker, Barbara Pym, Muriel Spark, Zora Neale Hurston, Wendy Wasserstein, Caryl Churchill, Jane Bowles, Maxine Hong Kingston and Faye Weldon. And this is only a preliminary list. Even if Mr. Bloom doesn't explode into laughter, he might at least learn to see the pie before it hits him in the face.

Audrey Bilger
Assistant Professor
Claremont McKenna College

NOTES ON CONTRIBUTORS

FICTION

Carolyn Cooke's work has appeared recently in *The Gettysburg Review*, *The American Voice* and *Puckerbrush Review*. She lives in California.

Guy Davenport's upcoming collection of stories, *The Cardiff Team*, will be published by New Directions this fall. He is a professor emeritus at the University of Kentucky at Lexington.

Jonathan Franzen is the author of the novels *The Twenty-Seventh City* and *Strong Motion*. He lives in New York City.

Ben Sonnenberg is the author of *Lost Property, Memoirs & Confessions of a Bad Boy*. He is the former editor and publisher of *Grand Street*.

POETRY

A.R. Ammons is the subject of an interview in this issue.

Claes Andersson is Finland's Minister of Culture and of Sport as well as the author of seventeen collections of poems, most recently *What Became Words*. His translator, **Rika Lesser**, is the author of three books of poems and the 1996 recipient of the Translation Prize of the Swedish Academy.

Ansie Baird's poems have appeared in such journals as *The Southern Review*, *Poetry Now* and *The Quarterly*. She lives in Buffalo.

Katherine Beasley is a professor of English at Tomball College. Her poetry has appeared in *Poetry Northwest* and *Slipstream*.

George Bradley's books include *The Fire Fetched Down* and *Terms to Be Met*, the latter chosen for the Yale Younger Poets Series.

Fred Dings is the author of *After the Solstice*, a collection of poems. He lives in West Chester, Pennsylvania.

Mark Doty is the author of *Turtle, Swan, Bethlehem in Broad Daylight, My Alexandria*, which won the National Book Critics Circle Award in 1993, and *Atlantis*. A memoir, *Heaven's Coast*, was published recently.

Serena J. Fox is an acute-care physician in Washington, D.C. Her work has appeared in *The Squaw Review*.

Joel Friederich's work has appeared recently in *Poetry Northwest* and *Tar River Review*. He lives in Japan.

Philip Hodgins published six volumes of poetry in Australia before his death in 1995. A seventh volume, *Things Happen*, appeared posthumously.

Rob House's work has appeared in *Southern Plains Review* and is forthcoming in *Western Humanities Review*. He lives in Houston.

Paul Kane's recent work includes a critical study, *Australian Poetry: Romanticism & Negativity* and an anthology, *Poetry of the American Renaissance*.

Carolyn Kizer, a chancellor of the Academy of American Poets, is the author, most recently, of *Picking and Choosing*, collection of essays. *Harping On*, a collection of poetry, is forthcoming. She recently edited *100 Great Poems by Women*.

James Laughlin's books include *Heart Island*, a collection of his epigrams, and *The Country Road*, a forthcoming collection of poetry. He founded New Directions Press.

David Lehman interviewed A.R. Ammons for this issue.

James Longenbach's poems have appeared in *The Best American Poetry 1995*. He won the 1995 *Nation*/Discovery Prize. The poem that appears in this issue was misprinted in issue 138; the correct version has been reprinted here.

Robin Magowan's books include *Fabled Cities of Central Asia, And Other Voyages, Burning the Knife* and *Tour de France*, which will be published this fall.

Gary Mitchner is a professor of English at Sinclair Community College. His poetry has appeared in *The Best American Poetry 1991*.

Jacqueline Osherow is the author of three books of poems: *Conversations with Survivors, Looking for Angels in New York* and the forthcoming *With a Moon in Transit*. She is an associate professor of English at the University of Utah.

Eric Pankey's fourth collection of poems, *This Reliquary World*, will be published next year. He is also the author of *For the New Year, Heartwood* and *Apocrypha*. He lives in St. Louis.

Alan Shapiro's most recent books are *Mixed Company*, a collection of poems, and *The Last Happy Occasion*, a memoir. He directs the Phoenix Poetry Series for the University of Chicago Press.

Phillip Sterling's poems have appeared in *The Georgia Review, The Kenyon Review* and *Western Humanities Review*. He is a professor of English at Ferris State University in Big Rapids, Michigan.

John Voiklis is currently in Greece working on a translation project for the
European Union Commission on Primary Education.
Liam Weitz has published poems in *Western Humanities Review*, *The Worm-
wood Review* and *Amazing Stories*. He teaches at the University of Houston.
David Yezzi reviews poetry for *Parnassus*. He lives in New York.

FEATURES

John Hopkins's *The Tangier Diaries 1962–1979*, from which the feature in
this issue is adapted, will be published this fall. He lives in England.
James Lord is the author of *Giacometti: A Biography*, *Picasso and Dora*,
A Giacometti Portrait and *Six Exceptional Women*. He lives in Paris.

INTERVIEWS

David Lehman (A.R. Ammons interview) is the author of *Valentine Place*,
a collection of poems, and *The Big Question*, a collection of essays.
Valerie Miles (Camilo José Cela interview) lives in Barcelona, where she
contributes to the cultural section of *La Vanguardia*.
Sam Vaughan (William F. Buckley interview) is Editor-at-Large at Random
House.

ART

Leona Christie is currently a resident at the MacDowell Colony. Her work
has been shown at Southern Exposure in San Francisco.
Philip Smith is represented by the Jason McCoy Gallery in New York City.
Donald Sultan's work is on exhibit at the Fotouhi Cramer Gallery in East
Hampton.

Errata

A number of errors cropped up in the last issue. A photograph of Terry
Southern (crouched in a phone booth) should have been identified as Jill
Krementz's. John Gregory Dunne's name was left off the spine by error,
and though a screenwriter of considerable repute, he would have been better
listed in the heading of his interview as a novelist. Peter Benchley was
described as the author of (along with *Jaws*) *How to Sleep*, a famous film
short starring his grandfather, Robert Benchley. If Peter had indeed been
responsible for *How to Sleep* he would be approaching his 105th year. In
Terry Southern's interview, the Pentagon is referred to as "viscous" rather
than "vicious," which might amuse Terry but surely not the copy editor.
Nathanael West gets an *i* instead of an *a*, which happens too often, and
Cincinnati turned up with too many *t*s. We will do better.

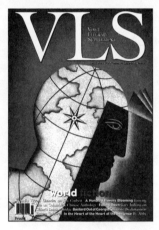

The Paris Review
Booksellers Advisory Board